I0821114

DEAD IN THE KITCHEN

DEAD IN THE KITCHEN

THE OFFICIAL **GRATEFUL DEAD** COOKBOOK

GABI MOSKOWITZ

FOREWORD BY MOLLIE KATZEN

weldonowen

CONTENTS

Side Players: Accompaniments

First Set: Quick, Casual Entrées

Riff Break: Improvisational Cooking

Second Set: Deeper, More Complex (But Not Complicated!) Entrées

Encore: Desserts

FOREWORD

BY MOLLIE KATZEN

A cultural era can seem simple in hindsight, especially to those who lived through, enjoyed, and fondly remembered the best of it. I'm thinking of this now, looking back from this present, more complex time, on the long musical moment of the Grateful Dead that was—and remains—so much more than tunes and rhythms. Through their music and ethos, the Dead brought us an evolving sound of hope, connection, invitation, inclusion. I lived through that time as a young, food-curious painter and classical musician—looking for, and often finding, connection among all the disciplines and ideas. I cooked to a self-curated soundtrack; I practiced the piano or played music while waiting for baked goods to emerge from the oven. As I stirred oats, nuts, and coconut together in the kitchen of my crowded-with-drop-ins apartment, then slid them onto a tray and into the oven to crisp (a concoction that would eventually become known as granola, but which was, at the time, just a new cereal-like mixture that a few other food people and I had begun making), the sounds of the Dead blared through my roommate's speakers in the next room. I'm sure a lot of people might associate the Grateful Dead with granola—after all, they're two of the best-known symbols of hippie culture—but for me, the connection was direct, and it lasts in all my fond associations to this day.

When the vegetarian-adjacent, internationally inspired, high-end restaurant where I worked in San Francisco would wind down its dinner shift late into the occasional Saturday evening, the chef and I ("pantry girl") would often cook a second round of dinner, this one to pack up and bring over to the Keystone Korner for Jerry Garcia's midnight jam. It felt amazing to feed those folks, and it also felt entirely kindred.

I loaded as many vegetables as I could grab from our walk-in refrigerator into the lasagnas we would deliver to the guys and their Grateful Dead–adjacent entourage, to eat in the back between sets. I thought about how those vegetables fueled and cheered the musicians and felt that somehow that resulting sound itself was the music of nourishment.

Yes, we were idealists. This kind of simplicity and sense of possibility pervaded our privileged, young lives, and I only wish that the new generations coming up in a darker, more complex world can get a sense of this too, by going back and listening to all the iterations of the Dead while pouring good olive oil over, let's say, a bowl of freshly cooked aromatic rice, infused with garlic and herbs, dotted with chickpeas, and singing the chorus of flavor and happiness.

The Dead's effect on the culture of the day—against the backdrop of the Vietnam War, the Civil Rights Movement and its immediate aftermath, the new Women's Liberation Movement, and the fledgling natural food "discoveries"—was strong. It was art and fun and meaning coming together to create community. As that community expanded, its unspoken emphasis on the idea of a Greater Good grew with it. The Dead taught us about freedom, kindness, selflessness, open-mindedness, compassion. As David Lemieux now reflects: "Just as we cared about others when we were on tour following and seeing the Dead in concert, we care about others now. The world around us, to all the Dead Heads I know, is interconnected, and isn't just about us. Our actions matter."

To understand that actions impact everything—and to act on that as much as we knew how—was a part of the overall zeitgeist. Those actions included, for lack of a more artful way to phrase it, "conscious lifestyle choices." (I add quotes because I find it quaint now, but in a beautiful way.) This notion dovetailed completely with our decisions about how and what to cook and eat, as we were looking backward to simpler, older ways of approaching sustenance, keeping in mind the earth, the environment, the cultures that came before, the creators upon whose shoulders we stood, realizing that much of these ideas were borrowed from ancient times, and seeing that as keeping alive something precious and true.

To enjoy spontaneous music combined with a joyfully prepared meal was always the top center goal of our daily lives. All our vitality went to create more vitality. All of our creative choices (poppy seeds for me, maybe, and edgy chords for/from the musicians) made a weave that became our lives. Our hope? That our choices would affect ourselves and others positively, that we could tread lightly (if not noisily) upon the earth, that everything was both expansive and finite, that we contain within us the ability to make things better for others, even if only a little bit.

I hope and trust you will now blast your music, roll up your sleeves, and cook a simple feast for you and your loved ones. This is an everlasting possibility in our lives—one we can make happen in every era.

WELCOME TO THE SHOW

As any lifelong Dead Head will tell you, being a devotee of the Grateful Dead is about a lot more than loving the music. It's more than knowing the rising and moon signs of every member by heart, and even more than being able to recite the Dead's 1977 tour schedule backward and forward. Being a Dead Head means belonging to a tightly knit community with long-standing traditions and a unique, pervasive culture that extends far beyond the music. Like any culture, the values, beliefs, and preferences of Dead Heads are reflected in its art, clothing, and language. If you've ever wandered through a venue parking lot before a show and seen the plethora of Stealie bumper stickers and handmade tie-dyed T-shirts, heard the word *kind* more times and in more ways than you knew existed, or overheard more than one person wishing aloud for "a Miracle," you know that well. But more than anything else, you notice the delicious smells wafting through the air, mobile kitchen vendors serving up their specialties, and happy Dead Heads all around you, munching on something delicious to fuel the hours of dancing ahead. From the band's first show in a pizza parlor in Menlo Park, California, to their commitment to bringing a caterer on the road to accommodate each member's unique preferences, to the kind veggie burritos; vibrant curries cooked in giant pots balanced precariously on tiny hot plate burners; tuna melts, egg rolls the size of footballs oozing spicy-sweet sauce; garlic salt–crusted grilled cheeses; Grateful Dead and food have always gone hand in hand.

Before the 1960s and 1970s, few people in the United States were aware of so-called health foods like yogurt, alfalfa sprouts, tempeh, and tofu, but they became a mainstay of hippie culture, so many Dead Heads embraced them early on. Over time, they became an integrated part of the Dead show experience, as vendors brought them to the parking lot, and Dead Heads shared nutritious, communal vegetarian meals on the road, following the band from city to city.

In this book, you'll find recipes inspired by not only the Grateful Dead's music and ethos but also the Dead Head movement at large. One thing you won't find is meat. While vegetarianism certainly isn't a requirement of loving the Dead, it has historically been popular among Dead Heads (and a few of the band members). Whether inspired by the Dead's messages of compassion and connectedness, a need to keep one's food budget low while on the road, or just an especially delicious kind veggie burrito, eschewing meat has long been woven into Dead Head culture.

If you're new to plant-based cooking, rest easy. In addition to being healthy and animal friendly, the recipes in this book are simple, straightforward, and doable for everyone from novice cooks to seasoned kitchen pros. They don't require complicated equipment or techniques, and you can count on finding easy-to-source ingredients (with alternative options listed whenever possible), so you don't have to go running around to three different stores trying to find the right kind of cumin. Best of all, the results will please even your most carnivorous friends and family members, fellow Dead Heads or otherwise.

The Grateful Dead are well known for their unique approach to putting on a concert. Whether you spent your salad days following the band or you've only ever listened to recordings, this cookbook aims to help you get in the Dead-inspired cooking mood by conjuring the experience of attending a show through food. Once you get your Kind Kitchen all set up and note Sustainable Kitchen Products on the next few pages, you'll start in The Lot with recipes inspired by the most iconic dishes sold there before and after shows. Next up is The Dressing Room with recipes for sauces, dressings, and condiments, which can be used in recipes throughout the book. Things get going with the Opening Act chapter with recipes for little bites, snacks, and appetizers to whet your appetite for the main event, then we move on to Tuning Up, with soups and salads to give you a taste of what's to come, just as the band often did, playing a few notes here and there, tuning their instruments before the show. Side Players features side dishes that conjure the same element of surprise and excitement as guest musicians who sit in for a song or two at Dead shows.

The First Set dishes are simple and quick to prepare, just as the first set of a Dead show features shorter, faster songs. Between the first and second acts, we'll take a Riff Break—a chapter that walks you through the culinary version of what the Grateful Dead are perhaps best known for: improvisation. The Second Set chapter features recipes that are, while still approachable for cooks of all skill levels, a bit more effortful and time-consuming, like the longer, more intense songs played in the second half of a show. In Encore, desserts are front and center. That may end the show, but you don't have to go home yet because it's time for the Afterparty—with curated picks by the Dead's longtime archivist David Lemieux and guidance on sourcing ingredients.

So, pull on your brightest tie-dye, crank up your favorite Dead album, and let's get cooking. These recipes are designed to be easy for cooks of all skill sets, so you're sure to have no trouble following them, but if, in the process, you should find yourself lost along the way, just close your eyes and let the music lead you back.

THE KIND KITCHEN

Kindness is a theme throughout much of the Dead's music, and the word *kind* has come to hold great meaning for Dead Heads, in reference to the character trait, veggie burritos, and more. In this book, a kind kitchen is one that reflects the eating habits and values of many Dead Heads: kind to animals (mostly or entirely plant based) and kind to the earth (as sustainable as possible). Here are the pantry, fridge, and freezer staples to set you up for animal-friendly cooking success, along with a few environmentally friendly kitchen tools and techniques to help extend all that kitchen kindness to Mother Earth.

PANTRY

RICE AND OTHER GRAINS: It's great to have a variety of white and brown rice types, such as long-grain basmati, short-grain Calrose, forbidden black, sushi rice, and more, but if you want to buy only one, get a medium-grain rice such as jasmine, which will work well in most recipes. Quinoa, couscous (fine grain and pearl types), bulgur, farro, barley, and kasha are also nice to have on hand.

DRIED NOODLES AND PASTA: Last-minute meals come together in a snap when you have a well-stocked pasta collection: short and long cuts of pasta like penne, bowtie, elbow macaroni, rigatoni, fusilli, spaghetti, linguine, fettuccine, and a variety of Asian noodles, such as soba, udon, rice vermicelli, and pad Thai, and rice paper spring roll wrappers.

BEANS AND LENTILS: Both canned and dried beans and legumes are excellent sources of protein and fiber—not to mention extremely cheap.

VEGETABLE BROTH AND/OR BOUILLON: Saving your veggie scraps to make homemade broth or stock is always a good idea, but when you don't have the time (or storage space), broth in cans or cartons or bouillon powders and concentrates are an excellent alternative.

CANNED TOMATO PRODUCTS: Whole, crushed, and diced tomatoes are useful in a huge variety of recipes, and tomato paste is an ideal way to inject a dish with intense tomato flavor. Squeezable tomato paste tubes are a mess-free way to use only what you need, but it also freezes well, so if you buy the canned variety, transfer leftovers into ice cube trays or an airtight container and store in the freezer for up to three months.

LOW-SODIUM SOY SAUCE OR TAMARI, COCONUT AMINOS: Opting for the lower-in-salt version of these umami-rich sauces gives you a little extra control of the flavor.

NUTS, SEEDS, AND NUT AND SEED BUTTERS: In general, it's best to opt for the raw (or blanched) version of a nut—you can always toast it at home. Whole and slivered or sliced almonds, pine nuts, sunflower seeds, pecans, walnuts, hemp seeds, flaxseeds, chia seeds, sesame seeds. Cashews, in particular, are an extremely useful nut to have on hand for plant-based cooking, since soaking and puréeing them with water or other liquids adds delicious dairy-like richness in everything from curries, soups, and dressings to vegan "cheesecakes" and ice creams.

OILS: Extra-virgin olive oil, virgin coconut oil, avocado oil, grapeseed oil, and toasted sesame oil.

VINEGARS: White distilled vinegar for pickling (and cleaning!), rice vinegar, apple cider vinegar, balsamic vinegar, and red wine vinegar.

CANNED COCONUT MILK AND CREAM: Equally excellent in Thai and Indian curries, or as the stand-in for dairy milk or cream in everything from pasta sauces to coconut caramel to vegan whipped cream.

SPICE RACK

* Aleppo pepper
* Ancho chile powder
* Basil
* Black pepper (preferably whole peppercorns ground just before using)
* Cardamom (pods or ground)
* Chili powder
* Chipotle chile powder
* Cinnamon
* Coriander
* Cumin (seeds or ground)
* Dried ginger
* Flaky sea salt (such as Maldon)
* Garlic powder
* Garlic salt
* Ground cloves
* Kosher salt
* Marjoram
* Nutmeg (fresh or ground)
* Onion powder
* Oregano
* Red pepper flakes
* Rosemary
* Sage
* Smoked paprika
* Sumac
* Sweet paprika
* Tarragon
* Thyme
* Turmeric
* Yellow curry powder

BAKING STAPLES

MAPLE SYRUP: Dark/robust maple syrup has a deeper maple flavor, whereas the golden/light variety provides sweetness with less of a maple punch. Be sure to buy real maple syrup, not "pancake syrup" or other artificially flavored syrups. Maple syrup can be pricey though, so sugar (brown, white granulated, or coconut) may be used in its place. Or, if you are not a strict vegan, honey may be used as well.

VANILLA EXTRACT OR PASTE: Use the extract when you want just a kiss of vanilla bean flavor, and the paste, which is generally more intensely flavored, when you want it to be more pronounced.

UNSWEETENED OR DUTCH PROCESS COCOA POWDER: For everything from brownies to savory sauces and chiles.

SUGARS: Coconut sugar, brown sugar, granulated sugar, confectioners' sugar. Be sure to look for brands labeled "Sucanat," which is short for "sugar cane natural," "beet sugar," or "whole cane sugar" if you are a strict vegan, as some white granulated sugar and confectioners' sugar brands are processed using bone char, an animal derivative used for whitening.

BLANCHED ALMOND FLOUR (NOT ALMOND MEAL): A wonderful low-carb, gluten-free flour for cookies, quick breads, and pancakes. Once you've opened the bag, transfer it to an airtight container and store in the freezer for up to six months.

GRAIN FLOURS: All-purpose, whole wheat, rye, and spelt flours are terrific for most baking projects. Quinoa flour, white and brown rice flours, and teff flour are flavorful gluten-free options and may also be added to wheat-based flours for flavor and texture. If you want to make a wheat flour–based recipe gluten-free, opt for a 1:1 baking flour, such as the Cup4Cup and Bob's Red Mill brands, which may be used just like regular all-purpose flour in baking recipes.

EGG REPLACER OR GROUND FLAXSEED: For replacing eggs in baked goods. To prepare a flax egg, stir together 1 tablespoon ground flaxseeds (be sure they're ground—whole seeds won't work) with 3 tablespoons water and let the mixture sit for 10 to 15 minutes, until it begins to congeal.

TAPIOCA STARCH AND CORNSTARCH: Great for thickening sauces, soups, and stir-fries.

BAKING POWDER AND BAKING SODA: For leavening cookies, cakes, flour tortillas, and more.

INSTANT YEAST: Instant yeast does not need to be dissolved or activated prior to using. Just mix it in with the dry ingredients and let it do its thing.

SEMISWEET OR DARK CHOCOLATE CHIPS, CHUNKS, OR BARS: If you're vegan or dairy-free, be sure to buy the kind marked as such (many chocolate products contain milk or milk by-products, even if they're not labeled as milk chocolate).

2.5 cc.
1/4 teaspoon
1.25 cc.

SUSTAINABLE KITCHEN PRODUCTS

SILICONE STORAGE BAGS: These are a bit pricier than the plastic baggies you use and throw away, but they're an investment that pays off in a big way, as these zip-able bags may be reused hundreds of times, and many brands can even go in the dishwasher for super-easy cleanup. They're great for your wallet and even better for the earth.

BEESWAX WRAP: Though not strictly vegan—they are made from thin cloth dipped in beeswax—beeswax wraps are an excellent alternative to the sheets upon sheets of plastic wrap or foil you might use to cover a dish of leftovers before refrigerating, wrap a sandwich, or preserve the unused half of an onion so it stays fresh in the veggie bin until you need it next. If you prefer a completely animal-free reusable wrap, look for candelilla wax wraps, which are made using a plant-based wax derived from the leaves of the small candelilla shrub.

SILICONE BAKING MATS: Like silicone storage bags, these smooth, slippery sheets of silicone, which are generally cut to fit the bottom of baking sheets, effectively replace their single-use counterparts—parchment paper and foil in this case. The most common brand is Silpat, but many other brands exist. You can even find ones with cookie shapes and measurement lines printed on them to guide you as you bake.

REUSABLE "PAPER" TOWELS: Paper towel alternatives, usually made from a combination of cotton and/or microfiber and cellulose, are absorbent fiber towels, often packaged in a roll, that are great for quickly wiping up small spills, just as you would with regular paper towels, except these may be reused and washed dozens of times. For an even longer-lasting, lower-environmental-impact option, cut old terrycloth towels or linen shirts into squares, roll or fold them, and keep in a basket on your kitchen counter. When soiled, just wash, dry, and reuse.

REUSABLE STRAWS: There's just something about drinking a glass of fresh juice, a delicious smoothie, or an iced latte through a straw that makes it taste better—but as you probably know, the impact of disposable plastic straws on the environment, especially ocean life, is detrimental. The good news is that reusable plastic, silicone, metal, and glass straws give you the disposable straw experience without the harm, which means they're good for you and good for the turtles.

CLEANING PRODUCTS FROM YOUR KITCHEN CUPBOARD: Many grocery staples can also be used to naturally and effectively clean your house. Here's a list of items you probably already have on hand that are good for more than just cooking:

- **Distilled White Vinegar:** Mix a 1:1 solution of vinegar and water in a spray bottle and use it to remove stains, kill bacteria, and clean surfaces. Add ½ cup to your washing machine's rinse cycle for an allergy-friendly fabric softener alternative.
- **Baking soda:** Make a thick, gently abrasive cleaning paste by adding a few pinches of baking soda to water or vinegar to easily clean baked-on food from pots and pans and remove stains from glass, tile, and ceramic.
- **Kosher salt:** Rub a palmful over the bottom of your cast-iron frying pan to loosen any debris that couldn't be removed with a sponge or to thoroughly clean your cutting board, or use a halved raw potato.
- **Olive oil:** A good scrub followed by a thin coating of oil gives new life to stainless steel and cast-iron pots and pans. Or mix 1 cup olive oil with ½ cup lemon juice to make an effective furniture polish for hardwood furniture.
- **Lemons:** The natural acidic properties of lemons make them great for cleaning. Cut a lemon in half and cover the cut side in baking soda. Then use it to scrub your sink for a biodegradable, effective, deodorizing clean.

THE LOT

DISHES INSPIRED BY PARKING LOT FARE

A Grateful Dead concert might have a scheduled start time, but as any Dead Head will tell you, the Dead show *experience* starts much earlier in the day, in the parking lot, where a whole lot more than car parking happens.

The lot is a bustling, makeshift marketplace where fans can imbibe a variety of different preshow refreshments and peruse the tiny temporary storefronts of tie-dye artists, bootleg tape dealers, bumper sticker makers, and more. It isn't just about commerce—it's a place to catch up with old friends and meet new ones, to party and play. One might find hair braiding, hacky sack, and an awful lot of patchouli wafting through the air. But alongside it is the aroma of what many say is the heart and soul of the scene: the food.

Within the confines of the venue's parking lot, one can find a diverse, impromptu grassroots street food haven where concertgoers grab a bite before the show or satisfy post-show hunger before going home—or following the band to the location of their next show. The food is as varied as the crowd, often prepared on hot plates or mini grills in the back of a van by fellow Dead Heads and reflects the ethos of the scene—it's homemade, affordable, and often shared. Eating in the lot means participating in an unspoken agreement of mutual support, where fans aren't just consumers but also contributors to the vibrant, self-sustaining culture.

An ideal preshow lot meal is portable and easy to eat on the go; filling, so as to fuel hours of dancing; and cheap. The recipes in this chapter aren't based on specific vendors—the book *Cooking with the Dead* by Elizabeth Zipern is a wonderful collection of recipes directly from the vendors themselves—but rather are plant-based interpretations of some of the lot's greatest hits. Whether you make them at home or cook them over a camping stove in a parking lot, these dishes will give you the distinct feeling that a very, very good time is about to begin.

KIND VEGGIE BEAN AND CHEESE BURRITOS

A "kind" veggie burrito is more than just a typical vegetarian burrito; it embodies the generous, laid-back, and communal vibe of places like the lot and Dead shows in general. "Kind" in this context refers to something that's wholesome, made with love, and shared with good intentions. This burrito may look basic from the outside, but after one bite, you'll find that the textures and flavors within are the very definition of *kind*.

YIELD: 4 BURRITOS

One 15-ounce can black or pinto beans, drained and rinsed

½ cup water

½ teaspoon kosher salt

½ teaspoon garlic powder

4 large (10-inch) white or whole wheat flour tortillas (Whole Wheat Tortillas/Flatbread on page 117 make these extra special) or use rice flour tortillas for a gluten-free burrito

4 ounces jack or cheddar cheese, grated (use your favorite vegan shreds or dip, like Better Cheddar Vegan Cheese Dip on page 74, for a vegan burrito)

2 cups prepared Tomato Rice (page 105)

1 large or 2 medium tomatoes, seeded and chopped (about ½ cup chopped)

½ medium red or white onion, finely chopped (about ½ cup chopped)

1 large handful fresh cilantro leaves and stems, finely chopped (about ½ cup chopped)

¼ cup sour cream, plain Greek yogurt (dairy or plant based), or Cashew Crema (page 46)

1 avocado, peeled, halved, pitted, and sliced or cubed

Hot sauce, to taste (optional)

In a small pot, combine the beans with the water, salt, and garlic powder and cook over medium heat for 5 to 6 minutes, just until heated through. Alternatively, heat in a microwave-safe bowl in the microwave on high power for 1½ minutes (cover the bowl with a damp paper towel so the beans don't explode), until heated through. Drain any excess water.

To assemble a burrito, lay a tortilla on a flat surface and sprinkle with one-fourth of the cheese in an even layer. Top with ½ cup beans; ½ cup rice; 2 tablespoons each of chopped tomato, onion, cilantro, and sour cream or yogurt; a few slices of avocado; and hot sauce if desired. Roll tightly, making sure to tuck in the ends.

Heat a large frying pan over high heat (do not add oil or butter to the pan). Cook the rolled burrito for 1 to 2 minutes on each side to sear lightly.

Serve the burritos sliced in half on a plate or wrap tightly in foil and eat on the go. Serve any remaining rice on the side.

KIND SHAWARMA-SPICED CAULIFLOWER BURRITOS

These flavorful, filling shawarma-spiced veggie wraps, while not traditional burritos, would be perfect for a Dead show tailgate. Serving at home? Pass the hummus, tahini, and other toppings for self-assembly. For takeout, assemble, roll tightly, and wrap in foil to keep warm (delicious cold too). The shawarma spice blend works well on any roastable vegetable, or cubed/crumbled tofu, tempeh, or seitan. Double or triple the blend and store unused mix in an airtight jar for future use.

YIELD: 4 BURRITOS

FOR THE CAULIFLOWER

1 large head cauliflower, trimmed and cut into 1-inch pieces

3 tablespoons extra-virgin olive oil

½ teaspoon kosher salt

A few grinds black pepper

¼ teaspoon ground cumin

½ teaspoon ground turmeric

½ teaspoon ground coriander

½ teaspoon garlic powder

½ teaspoon smoked paprika

Pinch ground cloves

A few dashes cayenne pepper, or more to taste

FOR THE TAHINI SAUCE

2 tablespoons well-stirred tahini

Juice of 1 lemon

2 tablespoons water

1 clove garlic, finely minced

Kosher salt and freshly ground black pepper

FOR ASSEMBLY

4 large (10-inch) white or whole wheat flour tortillas

½ cup Classic Hummus (page 66) or Carrot-Lentil Hummus, (page 64)

1 ripe avocado, peeled, halved, pitted, and sliced

2 tablespoons Quick-Pickled Onions (page 41)

2 cups labneh, plain Greek or nondairy yogurt, or Cashew Crema (page 46)

Chopped tomatoes and/or cucumber (optional)

Preheat the oven to 425°F.

To make the cauliflower: Combine the cauliflower, oil, salt, black pepper, and spices in a large mixing bowl. Toss well to coat.

Spread the cauliflower on a rimmed baking sheet and roast for 25 to 30 minutes, stirring occasionally, until the cauliflower has browned and is tender.

Meanwhile, to make the tahini sauce: Whisk together the tahini, lemon juice, water, garlic, and salt and black pepper to taste in a small bowl. Set aside.

To assemble a burrito: Warm or lightly grill the tortillas to make them pliable. Spread a tortilla with one-fourth of the hummus. Layer on one-fourth of the cauliflower, a good drizzle of the tahini sauce, one-fourth of the avocado, one-fourth of the pickled onions, and one-fourth of the labneh. Roll tightly, tucking in the ends so the fillings don't fall out, and serve on plates or wrap in foil for a portable option.

KIND BULGUR BURRITOS WITH MINTY CABBAGE SLAW

Nutty, high-fiber wheat bulgur stands in for the usual rice in this burrito that puts the "veggie" in "kind veggie burrito," though any other cooked grain will work. For a gluten-free version, try quinoa or amaranth. The broccoli may also be swapped for other dense veggies, such as cauliflower, carrots, or diced sweet potatoes.

YIELD: 4 BURRITOS

FOR THE SLAW

½ small head red cabbage, thinly sliced

½ medium red onion, thinly sliced

1 carrot, shredded

1 large handful fresh mint, chopped (about ¼ cup chopped)

3 tablespoons seasoned rice vinegar

FOR THE BURRITOS

1 cup bulgur

2 cups water

½ teaspoon kosher salt

2 tablespoons extra-virgin olive oil

½ medium red onion, diced

2 cloves garlic, minced

1 small head broccoli, cut into small florets

One 15-ounce can black beans, drained and rinsed

4 large (10-inch) white or whole wheat flour tortillas (Whole Wheat Tortillas/Flatbread on page 117 make these extra special) or use rice flour tortillas for a gluten-free option

4 ounces jack or cheddar cheese, grated (use your favorite vegan shreds or dip, like Better Cheddar Vegan Cheese Dip on page 74, for a vegan burrito)

To make the slaw: In a large bowl, toss together the cabbage, sliced onion, carrot, mint, and vinegar. Set aside.

To make the burritos: In a small pot, bring the bulgur and water to a boil over high heat. Stir, cover, reduce the heat to medium-low, and cook for 8 to 10 minutes, or until all the water is absorbed. Sprinkle with the salt and fluff with a fork. Set aside.

In a medium frying pan over medium heat, heat the oil. Add the diced onion and the garlic. Cook for 1 minute, stirring frequently. Add the broccoli and cook for 2 to 3 minutes, until tender but still crisp. Stir in the beans and cook just until they are hot. Turn off the heat and cover the pan.

Heat a large, dry frying pan over high heat. While it heats up, lay a tortilla on a flat surface. Layer with one-fourth of the cheese, bulgur, and bean-vegetable mixture. If eating on the go, add a few spoonfuls of the slaw. Roll up the tortilla tightly, tucking in the ends. Cook, seam side down, in the dry pan until the tortilla becomes crisp and brown. Flip over and cook the top. This will also help melt the cheese.

Serve hot on a plate with the slaw on the side if eating at home or wrapped tightly in foil if eating on the go.

GARLIC-CRUSTED BLACK BEAN QUESADILLAS

Crispy, cheesy triangles of goodness are extremely popular preshow choices and have the benefit of offering the satisfying, nutritious fillings usually available in burrito form (beans, veggies, cheese), with the gooeyness and crispy, garlicky packaging usually associated with grilled cheese, another favorite on the lot. Make these with just-shucked corn when it's in season and opt for frozen kernels the rest of the time.

YIELD: 4 SERVINGS

One 15-ounce can black beans, drained and rinsed

¾ cup fresh (from one medium ear of corn) or frozen corn kernels

⅓ large or 1 small red onion, diced

1 clove garlic, minced

¼ bunch fresh cilantro, chopped (about ½ cup chopped)

8 ounces cheddar or jack cheese, shredded (about 2 cups shredded; use your favorite vegan shreds or dip, like Better Cheddar Vegan Cheese Dip on page 74, for a vegan quesadilla)

½ teaspoon chili powder

⅛ teaspoon ground cumin

¼ teaspoon onion powder

¼ teaspoon kosher salt

4 large (10-inch) flour tortillas or Whole Wheat Tortillas/Flatbread (page 117), or 8 small (6-inch) corn tortillas

1 tablespoon avocado or grapeseed oil, plus more for the pan as needed

½ teaspoon garlic salt, plus more as needed

Add the black beans to a bowl with the corn (no need to thaw if using frozen). Add the onion, garlic, cilantro, cheddar, spices, and kosher salt to the beans and corn. Stir until everything is evenly combined and coated in the seasoning.

Lay the tortillas on a work surface. Divide the filling among the tortillas, placing the filling on one half of the tortilla. Fold the other half over the filling. Brush both sides with the oil and sprinkle lightly with the garlic salt.

Heat a large, heavy-bottomed frying pan over medium heat and add a bit more oil. Add one large or two small quesadillas to the pan and cover. Cook for about 1 minute, then uncover to determine if the bottom of the tortilla is crisp and the cheese has melted.

Flip the quesadilla with a spatula and cook until that side is brown and crispy and the cheese has melted. Slice into three triangles to serve.

FATTY EGG ROLLS

Scan a Dead lot at any time, and you'll see no shortage of people enjoying foil-wrapped cylinders of deliciousness as they mill about. Though many of those cylinders are sure to be kind veggie burritos of some sort, you'll likely find that a good many are these enormous crispy-skinned 8-inch cylinders filled with a mixture of bright, crunchy veggies, crumbled tofu, and a spicy-sweet sauce already inside, so there's no need to carry around an additional container.

YIELD: 6 LARGE EGG ROLLS

FOR THE EGG ROLLS

1 cup plus 1 tablespoon neutral oil, such as avocado or grapeseed oil, plus more as needed

1 red bell pepper, seeded and diced

4 green onions, sliced

1 large carrot, peeled and shredded

½ small or ¼ large head red or green cabbage, thinly sliced (about 4 cups sliced)

2 heads bok choy, thinly sliced (about 2 cups sliced)

3 cloves garlic, minced

1-inch piece fresh ginger, minced

3 ounces firm or extra-firm tofu, crumbled

2 tablespoons soy sauce, tamari, or coconut aminos

12 large square egg roll wrappers (wrapper sizes vary between brands, but you're looking for something 6½ to 8 inches square)

FOR THE SAUCE

¼ cup sweet-and-sour sauce

2 tablespoons sriracha, or more to taste

To make the egg rolls: Heat 1 tablespoon of the oil in a large, heavy-bottomed frying pan over medium heat. Add all the vegetables, including the garlic and ginger, and cook, stirring frequently, until quite fragrant and slightly soft, about 3 minutes. You're not looking for anything to be browned, just softened.

Add the tofu and soy sauce. Toss gently and cook for 1 minute. Transfer the mixture to a bowl and set aside to cool. Clean the frying pan for later use.

To make the sauce: Mix the sauce ingredients in a small bowl.

To assemble the egg rolls: Lay one egg roll wrapper on a clean, dry surface. Brush one edge lightly with water. Then lay a second wrapper on the moistened seam so it overlaps slightly and press to seal. Now you should have one long rectangular wrapper. Put one-sixth of the vegetable-tofu filling in a vertical mound in the middle of the wrapper and spoon 1 tablespoon of sauce over the filling. Tuck the ends of the wrapper in and roll up as tightly as possible, as though making a burrito.

Repeat with the remaining egg roll wrappers, filling, and sauce.

Pour about 1 inch of oil into the frying pan and heat over medium-high heat. Working in batches, cook the egg rolls, seam side down, until golden and crispy. Flip and cook on the other side. Add more oil to the pan if necessary. Drain on paper towels or a cooling rack.

Serve warm.

BAKED HEMP FALAFEL

Falafel is a perfect preshow food, thanks to the combination of complex carbohydrates and the hunger-fighting combination of plant-based protein and fiber. But throw in a hefty dose of hemp hearts, and you'll pack in an additional 10 grams of protein per serving, giving you energy to dance until the sun comes up should you choose to do so. Even better, these easy, flavorful falafels are baked instead of fried, making cleanup a snap.

YIELD: 4 SERVINGS

FOR THE FALAFEL

1 cup dried chickpeas

1¼ teaspoons kosher salt

1 cup fresh parsley, cilantro, and dill, finely chopped

1 small onion, minced

¾ cup hemp seed hearts

½ teaspoon cayenne pepper

FOR THE TAHINI SAUCE

2 tablespoons well-stirred tahini

Juice of 1 lemon

2 tablespoons water

1 clove garlic, finely minced

Kosher salt and freshly ground black pepper

FOR ASSEMBLY

4 pitas or Whole Wheat Tortillas/ Flatbread (page 117)

¼ cup Quick-Pickled Onions (page 41) or thinly sliced raw red onions

Chopped tomatoes and cucumber

Lemon wedges, for garnish

To make the falafel: Cover the dried chickpeas in a bowl with water and soak for 8 hours. Drain the chickpeas and combine with enough water to cover in a large pot with ½ teaspoon salt. Cover the pot and bring the water to a boil over high heat. Reduce the heat to low and simmer for 1½ to 2 hours, until tender. Drain and cool the chickpeas.

In a food processor, pulse the chickpeas with the herbs a few times, just to break down the chickpeas. Add the onion, hemp seed hearts, remaining ¾ teaspoon salt, and cayenne. Use a spoon or cookie scoop to shape into twelve to sixteen 1½-inch balls and chill in the refrigerator for 1 hour.

Preheat the oven to 450°F and line a baking sheet with a silicone baking mat or parchment paper.

Place the falafel on the prepared baking sheet. Bake for 15 to 20 minutes, until golden brown, flipping once halfway through.

To make the tahini sauce: In a small bowl, whisk together the tahini, lemon juice, water, garlic, and salt and pepper to taste. Set aside.

To assemble a falafel sandwich: Spread a pita with a drizzle of the tahini sauce. Top with two or three baked falafels and garnish with the pickled onion, tomatoes, and cucumber. Wrap tightly and serve.

TEMPEH SATAY WITH PEANUT SAUCE

Grilled food on a stick is a classic snack to eat before (or after) a Dead show, and for good reason: It's highly portable, sustaining, and tasty. This Thai-inspired take on the classic meat-on-a-stick dish satay is meat-free, but just as flavorful thanks to a long bath in a tangy peanut-coconut marinade before cooking. These are terrific with the peanut dipping sauce, but they're also nice with Coconut Rice (page 104) or tucked into butter lettuce leaves with fresh cilantro and sliced chiles.

YIELD: 24 SATAY STICKS

Two 10-ounce packages tempeh

1 recipe prepared Peanut Sauce (page 45)

Juice of 2 limes

2 teaspoons soy sauce, tamari, or coconut aminos

2 teaspoons ground turmeric

1 cup full-fat coconut milk

1 tablespoon maple syrup

1 to 2 tablespoons neutral oil, such as avocado or grapeseed oil

Chopped fresh cilantro and sliced jalapeños, for serving (optional)

If using bamboo skewers and a gas or charcoal grill, soak the skewers in water for at least 30 minutes.

Cut each tempeh into twelve 3-inch strips, about ¾ inch wide. Push the strips onto the tips of the skewers.

Combine ½ cup of the peanut sauce, lime juice, soy sauce, turmeric, coconut milk, and maple syrup in a 9-by-13-inch baking dish. Whisk well to incorporate, breaking up any lumps. Store the remaining peanut sauce in an airtight container in the refrigerator.

Add the skewers with the tempeh to the sauce and stir gently to cover them with the sauce. Cover the pan and marinate in the refrigerator for 12 to 24 hours.

Heat a grill or grill pan over medium-high heat. If using a grill pan, brush with the oil. Grill the tempeh for 2 to 3 minutes on each side, or until lightly crisp with grill marks.

Serve the satay sticks with the cilantro and jalapeños if desired and the remaining peanut sauce on the side for dipping. The refrigerated sauce may need to sit out on the counter for 30 to 60 minutes to return to a smooth, dippable consistency, but you may also whisk in a bit of water to thin it before serving.

HUMMUS AVOCADO WRAPS

Though not technically a burrito, this nutritious wrap shares the spirit of its kind veggie burrito brethren in that it's a portable tortilla cylinder full of vegetables and legumes. Consider the vegetables listed mere suggestions and don't hesitate to swap in your favorites.

YIELD: 4 WRAPS

4 Whole Wheat Tortillas/Flatbread (page 117)

1 cup hummus (Classic Hummus page 66, Carrot-Lentil Hummus, page 64, or store-bought)

1 cup alfalfa sprouts

2 small carrots, grated or cut into matchsticks

2 ripe avocados, peeled, halved, pitted, and sliced

½ medium red onion, thinly sliced

1 English cucumber or 2 mini Persian cucumbers, sliced lengthwise into ribbons

1 red bell pepper, seeded and thinly sliced

1 cup baby spinach, baby kale, or mixed greens

Kosher salt and freshly ground black pepper

Place a wrap on a clean, dry workspace. Spread one-fourth of the hummus over the top, then layer evenly with one-fourth each of the alfalafa sprouts, carrots, avocados, red onion, cucumber, bell pepper, and greens of choice.

Sprinkle with a pinch each of salt and pepper. Roll tightly, tucking in the ends. Repeat with the remaining wraps.

Cut in half and serve or wrap tightly in foil and take on the go.

GARLICKY GRILLED CHEESE (3 WAYS)

Ask any Dead Head about the preshow food offering most often spotted in the venue parking lot and you'll no doubt hear the words "grilled cheese." Depending on how many shows they've attended (and how many mobile kitchen–cooked, foil-wrapped grilled cheeses they've sampled), they might also tell you about the not-so-secret ingredient that sets Dead Head grilled cheeses apart from the rest: a garlic salt-gilded crust that turns even the simplest, cheapest grocery store sandwich bread into buttery garlic bread—in other words, an extremely delicious vehicle for melted cheese, whether dairy or plant based.

Below you'll find a recipe for the garlicky, cheesy classic sandwich, along with two riffs: one stuffed with smoky mushroom bacon, and another with roasted broccoli. It's important to use a light hand with the garlic salt, since cheese is inherently salty, and make sure to distribute it evenly across the bread. Once you make this, you'll likely want to make sure your spice rack is never without garlic salt, but if you happen to be fresh out, just mix three parts kosher salt to one part garlic powder and one part dried parsley.

YIELD: 1 SANDWICH

2 slices sandwich bread, preferably something sturdy, but use whatever you've got

2 tablespoons unsalted butter (dairy or plant based), at room temperature, or mayonnaise (regular or plant based)

⅛ teaspoon garlic salt

1½ ounces shredded or thinly sliced cheddar cheese (any sharpness you prefer), ¼ cup shredded American cheese, Better Cheddar Vegan Cheese Dip (page 74), or store-bought vegan cheese (shreds, slices, or dip)

Heat a large, heavy-bottomed frying pan over medium heat.

When the pan is hot, coat both slices of bread with butter on one side. Lightly sprinkle a pinch of garlic salt on each of the buttered sides. Place in the pan, buttered side down.

While the bread toasts, carefully divide the cheese between both slices of the bread in an even layer, covering the slices all the way to the edges.

Cover the pan for 1 minute to encourage the cheese to melt and the bread to toast, turning the heat down slightly as needed to avoid burning.

Lift the lid and confirm that the cheese is melting and the bottom of each slice of bread has begun to toast lightly in the pan. If the cheese and/or bread needs to cook a bit longer, cover the pan again and lift the lid every 30 seconds or so, until the cheese has melted and the bottom of the bread is golden brown.

Place one of the cheese-covered slices of bread on top of the other to make a sandwich.

Slice the sandwich in half if desired and serve immediately.

MUSHROOM BACON GARLICKY GRILLED CHEESE

Though it may be applied to any firm, low-moisture mushroom, king trumpet mushrooms (sometimes also called king oyster mushrooms) have the benefit of also being shaped more or less like pork bacon when you slice them lengthwise. While this recipe yields one sandwich, the mushroom bacon component is enough for four or more sandwiches. Use the extras for more sandwiches, serve with a tofu scramble, or snack on it by itself.

YIELD: 1 SANDWICH (WITH MUSHROOM BACON LEFTOVERS)

FOR THE MUSHROOM BACON

3 tablespoons extra-virgin olive oil

2 tablespoons brown or coconut sugar

½ teaspoon kosher salt

½ teaspoon smoked paprika

1 teaspoon freshly ground black pepper

2 large (or 3 or 4 smaller) king trumpet mushrooms, cut into bacon strip–size slices (about ⅛ inch thick)

¼ teaspoon liquid smoke

FOR THE SANDWICH

2 slices sandwich bread, preferably something sturdy, but use whatever you've got

2 tablespoons unsalted butter (dairy or plant based), at room temperature, or mayonnaise (regular or plant based)

⅛ teaspoon garlic salt

1½ ounces shredded or thinly sliced cheddar cheese (any sharpness you prefer), ¼ cup shredded American cheese, Better Cheddar Vegan Cheese Dip (page 74), or store-bought vegan cheese (shreds, slices, or dip)

Preheat the oven to 325°F.

To prepare the mushroom bacon: Lightly grease a rimmed 18-by-13-inch baking sheet with 1 tablespoon of the oil.

In a small bowl, stir together the brown sugar, salt, smoked paprika, and pepper. Set aside.

Place the mushrooms in a large mixing bowl. Drizzle with the remaining 2 tablespoons oil and the liquid smoke and toss well to combine.

Add the brown sugar mixture to the mushrooms and use your hands or a spoon to toss well, ensuring that each mushroom slice is well coated. Arrange the mushrooms in a single layer on the prepared baking sheet.

Bake for 18 to 22 minutes, until the mushrooms turn dark brown. Flip gently, using a spatula. Bake for another 15 to 17 minutes, until very brown. Let cool for at least 10 minutes (this will help the mushrooms crisp).

To prepare 1 sandwich: Heat a large, heavy-bottomed frying pan over medium heat. When the pan is hot, coat both slices of bread with butter on one side. Lightly sprinkle a pinch of garlic salt on each of the buttered sides. Place the bread in the pan, buttered side down.

While the bread toasts, carefully divide the cheese between both slices of the bread in an even layer, making sure to cover the slices all the way to the edges. Cover the pan for 1 minute to encourage the cheese to melt and the bread to toast, turning the heat down slightly as needed to avoid burning.

Lift the lid and confirm that the cheese is melting and the bottom of each slice of bread has begun to toast lightly in the pan. If the cheese and/or bread needs to cook a bit longer, cover the pan again and lift the lid every 30 seconds or so, until the cheese has melted and the bottom of the bread is golden brown. Arrange 4 to 6 slices of the mushroom bacon on one of the cheese-covered bread slices before covering with the second cheese-covered slice.

Flip the sandwich and cook with the lid off for another minute, until the cheese is nicely melted and the bread is golden brown and crisp on.

Slice the sandwich in half if desired and serve immediately.

MEAN GREEN GARLICKY GRILLED CHEESE

Roasted broccoli and green goddess dressing might seem like unorthodox additions to grilled cheese, but the final product is so full of umami goodness, crunchy and creamy textures, and welcome brightness, thanks to the green goddess, that you'll want to kick tradition to the curb and start putting broccoli and green goddess on every sandwich. Feel free to swap in other dense vegetables, like cauliflower, Romanesco broccoli, or broccoli rabe. And while fresh broccoli is called for in the recipe, frozen works just fine.

YIELD: 1 SANDWICH

FOR THE BROCCOLI

½ medium head broccoli (about ¼ pound), chopped, (about 1½ cups chopped)

1 tablespoon extra-virgin olive oil or avocado oil

Pinch kosher salt

A few grinds black pepper

3 tablespoons Vegan Green Goddess Dressing (page 47)

FOR THE SANDWICH

2 slices sandwich bread, preferably something sturdy, but use whatever you've got

2 tablespoons unsalted butter (dairy or plant based), at room temperature, or mayonnaise (regular or plant based)

⅛ teaspoon garlic salt

1½ ounces shredded or thinly sliced cheddar cheese (any sharpness you prefer), ¼ cup shredded American cheese, Better Cheddar Vegan Cheese Dip (page 74), or store-bought vegan cheese (shreds, slices, or dip)

Preheat the oven to 400°F.

To prepare the broccoli: On a sheet pan, toss the broccoli, oil, salt, and pepper with your hands or a rubber spatula. Roast for 8 to 10 minutes, or until the broccoli is nicely browned. Remove from the oven and let cool for 5 minutes (you don't want it to be cold—just not steaming). Toss the warm broccoli with 1 tablespoon of the dressing.

To prepare 1 sandwich: Heat a large, heavy-bottomed frying pan over medium heat.

Spread 1 tablespoon dressing on one side of each slice of bread, then coat both slices of bread with butter on the other side. Lightly sprinkle a pinch of garlic salt on each of the buttered sides and place both in the hot pan, buttered side down.

While the bread toasts, carefully divide the cheese between both slices of the bread in an even layer, covering the slices all the way to the edges, and spoon the dressed, roasted broccoli on one of the cheese-covered bread slices.

Cover the pan for 1 minute to encourage the cheese to melt and the bread to toast, turning the heat down slightly as needed to avoid burning.

Lift the lid and confirm that the cheese is melting and the bottom of each slice of bread has begun to toast lightly in the pan. If the cheese and/or bread needs to cook a bit longer, cover the pan again and lift the lid every 30 seconds or so, until the cheese has melted and the bottom of the bread is golden brown.

Place the cheese-covered slice of bread on top of the cheese-and-broccoli-covered one to make a sandwich. Carefully flip the sandwich (it's okay if you lose a few florets) and cook with the lid off for another minute, until the cheese is nicely melted and the bread is golden brown and crisp on both sides.

Slice the sandwich in half if desired and serve immediately.

HOT (NOT) TUNA MELTS

The Grateful Dead and Hot Tuna (originally founded as an acoustic spin-off of Jefferson Airplane) shared the stage on several occasions, during which audiences got to witness firsthand the magical combination of Hot Tuna's blues rock and the Dead's exploratory improvisation—a perfect blend of old-school and new-school styles. Whereas tuna salad might be the expected filling of this diner classic sandwich, the tuna melt gets a welcome update here, with lightly smashed chickpeas standing in for the tuna. Umami flavor bombs miso and Dijon mustard bring the briny, sea-inspired flavor without the need for actual fish, and the sandwich's usual suspects (buttered toasted bread, melted cheese, pickles) help keep it just grounded enough in tradition to be pleasantly familiar.

YIELD: 4 SANDWICHES

One 15-ounce can chickpeas

2 tablespoons mayonnaise (regular or plant based)

1 teaspoon Dijon mustard

1½ teaspoons miso paste

⅛ teaspoon sea salt

⅛ teaspoon freshly ground black pepper

1 to 2 tablespoons finely chopped red onion or Quick-Pickled Onions (page 41)

2 tablespoons sweet pickle relish

2 tablespoons leafy fresh herbs (e.g., dill, cilantro, parsley), finely chopped

One 8-by-8-inch sheet toasted nori (or equivalent), sliced into thin ribbons

2 tablespoons specify salted or unsalted butter (dairy or plant based), at room temperature

4 slices bread (8 for closed sandwiches), preferably something sturdy, such as Whole Wheat No-Knead Peasant Bread (page 111)

Four 1-ounce slices cheddar cheese (dairy or plant based)

Drain and rinse the chickpeas and pat them dry with a towel to remove excess liquid. Place them in a medium mixing bowl and use a potato masher or fork to mash them until there are no large pieces of chickpeas.

Add the mayonnaise, mustard, miso paste, salt, pepper, onion, relish, herbs, and nori and mix thoroughly.

Butter one side of each slice of bread as you heat a large, heavy-bottomed frying pan over medium heat. Once the pan is hot, place a slice of bread, butter side down, in the pan. Carefully top it with one-fourth of the chickpea mixture. Top the chickpea mixture with a slice of cheese and cover the pan. Cook the sandwich for 1 to 2 minutes, allowing the cheese to melt and occasionally checking the underside of the bread to make sure it isn't burning.

Optionally, top with a second piece of buttered bread, flip, and cook for another 2 to 3 minutes, until both sides are golden brown and crispy and the cheese has melted.

Repeat with the remaining bread, cheese, and chickpea mixture and serve hot.

THE DRESSING ROOM

DRESSINGS, SAUCES, AND CONDIMENTS

The band members' dressing rooms aren't accessible to concertgoers, but for the musicians, they play an important role: Dressing rooms are a space to get ready to perform in the physical, emotional, and spiritual senses. For musicians, the dressing room serves as something of an anchor for the whole show, and the same is true for the recipes in this chapter. While you may think of dressings as add-ons and enhancements, often they serve as an anchor, and can help make a dish sing.

For that reason, the dressings, sauces, and condiments in this chapter appear throughout this book. If you want to start cooking your way through this book but are unsure where to begin, this chapter is a great place, since a kitchen full of ready-to-go flavorings makes cooking not only easier but also a pleasure.

Many of these recipes call for a blender or food processor. If you don't have one, you can get similar (though not identical) results with a mortar and pestle and a little elbow grease. If you're interested in purchasing a blender or food processor but don't want to spend a lot of money, consider an immersion blender. Even the higher-end ones tend to be cheaper than standard full-size blenders and food processors, and they can be used to mix, purée, emulsify, chop, and whisk directly in the pot, bowl, or other container, making them ideal for saving both space and money.

LEAFY GREEN RELISH

This versatile, lightly spicy, herbaceous green sauce lies somewhere between Middle Eastern green schug (a spicy condiment usually made of fresh parsley and cilantro, garlic, fresh chiles, lemon juice, and spices) and Indian and Pakistani cilantro and/or mint chutneys. Try it on the Baked Hemp Falafel on page 27, the Baked Samosas on page 62, the Kind Shawarma-Spiced Cauliflower Burritos on page 21, and the Spicy Chickpea Curry on page 135. Drizzle it over tacos, roasted vegetables, or fries, or just swirl it into yogurt and serve it with chips or fresh bread for an easy and tasty dip.

YIELD: ABOUT 1¼ CUPS

2 medium serrano chiles or jalapeños (remove seeds and membrane for a milder sauce, or keep intact for a spicier one), or 1 to 2 teaspoons crushed red pepper flakes

3 garlic cloves, smashed with the back of a knife

1 1-inch piece ginger, peeled and roughly chopped

1½ cups lightly packed cilantro leaves and stems

1½ cups lightly packed flat-leaf parsley leaves and stems

1 cup lightly packed fresh mint leaves and stems

Zest and juice of 1 medium lemon

1 teaspoon ground coriander

½ teaspoon ground cumin

½ teaspoon ground cardamom

½ teaspoon kosher salt, or more to taste

¼ teaspoon freshly ground black pepper

½ cup extra-virgin olive oil

Put the chiles, garlic, and ginger in a food processor or blender and pulse to chop finely, then add the herbs, lemon zest and juice, spices, salt, and pepper.

Continue pulsing until the herbs are all very finely chopped and a thick puree is beginning to form, then stream in the oil with the machine running.

The sauce will keep for up to 1 week in an airtight container in the fridge.

SPICY-CRUNCHY CHILI OIL

If, like many Dead Heads, you've ever been called "crunchy," this recipe is your sign to take it as a compliment. Whereas most chili oils simply add flavor—specifically heat—this one also adds texture by way of crispy fried onions, garlic, and red pepper flakes. The list of foods this oil *doesn't* taste good on is shorter than the list of those that it does. Toss it with hot noodles, add it to a bowl of hummus, stir it into guacamole, drag dumplings through it, drizzle it over eggs, dip slices of pizza in it, or add it to a grilled cheese sandwich—or literally any sandwich. It's even good—if you can believe it—spooned over ice cream.

YIELD: ABOUT ¾ CUP

⅔ cup neutral oil, such as avocado or grapeseed oil

3 shallots or 1 medium onion, finely chopped (about 1 cup chopped)

1 tablespoon red pepper flakes

3 tablespoons dried minced garlic

1 teaspoon kosher salt

1 teaspoon paprika

Combine the oil and shallots in a small saucepan over medium-low heat. Cook, stirring occasionally, until the shallots are crispy and golden brown, about 15 minutes. Check frequently to avoid burning and turn down the heat as needed. Turn off the heat and stir in the red pepper flakes, dried garlic, salt, and paprika.

Let cool completely and transfer to an airtight glass jar or other container with a fitted lid, and store in the refrigerator for up to 1 month.

QUICK-PICKLED ONIONS

Even if you don't consider yourself an onion fan, you're likely to enjoy these crunchy, juicy-sweet, pickled ones. Use them anywhere you'd use fresh onions, such as on veggie burgers, in tacos, in salads, on enchiladas, or even finely chopped and added, along with a bit of their pickling liquid and some fresh herbs, to mayonnaise for a creamy, tangy sauce that's perfect for everything from carrot sticks to fries. This method may also be used to pickle just about any firm vegetable, such as thinly sliced cabbage, hot peppers, whole garlic cloves, radishes, carrots, and asparagus.

YIELD: ABOUT 2½ CUPS

1 cup distilled white vinegar

1 cup red wine vinegar

¼ cup sugar

2 tablespoons kosher salt

1 cup water

2 medium red onions, thinly sliced

In a medium pot, combine the vinegars, sugar, salt, and water. Whisk to combine, then cover, set the pot over high heat, and bring to a boil. Turn off the heat, add the onions, and let sit for 15 minutes.

Pour the onions and brine into a jar or other container and let cool to room temperature. The onions may be used once they are cool, but they'll taste better after a little time in the refrigerator.

Cover the container tightly and refrigerate until ready to use. The onions will keep in the refrigerator for up to 3 weeks.

ROMESCO SAUCE

Silky, smoky, lightly sweet romesco sauce may be Spanish in origin (if you've ever been to a tapas restaurant, you've likely been served crispy potatoes bathed in it), but it's good on just about anything from sandwiches to pasta, vegetables, fresh bread, and cooked grains, or even thinned with a bit of red wine vinegar to make a deliciously unique salad dressing. While most recipes call for a slice of stale bread to be puréed along with the other ingredients, this one leaves it out, making it both vegan and gluten-free. It freezes exceptionally well, so you can make a big batch and save whatever you don't use for a rainy day.

YIELD: ABOUT 4 CUPS

One 16-ounce jar roasted red peppers

One 15-ounce can diced tomatoes (preferably fire roasted)

3 cloves garlic, roughly chopped

½ cup toasted sliced or slivered almonds

1 handful fresh parsley, chopped (about 2 tablespoons chopped)

⅓ cup extra-virgin olive oil

¼ teaspoon smoked paprika, or more to taste

Freshly cracked black pepper

½ teaspoon kosher salt

Drain the roasted peppers, but reserve about 2 tablespoons of the vinegar. Purée the roasted peppers, the reserved vinegar, and all the other ingredients using a food processor, blender, or immersion blender until very smooth.

Use the sauce immediately (see the headnote for suggestions) or store in an airtight container for up to a week. Alternatively, freeze for up to 3 months.

COCONUT-CURRY DRESSING

This bright yellow, silky-smooth, lightly sweet, and just-spicy-enough dressing is perfect on everything from cold rice noodles to steamed vegetables, shaved cabbage, roasted sweet potatoes, and more. The raw cashews give the dressing much-needed body, but you may also substitute 2 tablespoons of tahini for a dressing that is different but also quite good.

YIELD: ABOUT 1 CUP

2 tablespoons raw cashews

1 cup full-fat coconut milk

¼ cup rice vinegar

Zest and juice of 2 limes

1 large handful fresh cilantro leaves and stems

2 cloves garlic, smashed

1-inch piece fresh ginger, chopped

1½ teaspoons yellow curry powder

1 to 2 tablespoons sriracha, depending on taste

1 to 2 tablespoons maple syrup or honey, depending on taste

Put the cashews in a small bowl and cover with boiling water. Cover the bowl with a fitted lid or a clean kitchen towel and let the cashews soak for 15 minutes. Drain the cashews.

Put all the ingredients in a blender or food processor and purée on high speed until very smooth.

Use immediately or store in an airtight container in the refrigerator for up to a week.

PEANUT SAUCE

There are practically as many varieties of peanut sauce as there are bootleg tapes of Dead shows on eBay, so calling this one "peanut sauce" as if it's some sort of prototype is slightly misleading. This sauce takes cues from both Thai and Vietnamese peanut sauce styles and is highly customizable, so feel free to give it your own personal spin. Don't like cilantro? Leave it out or try a few sprigs of fresh mint. It will taste different but still very good. All out of rice vinegar? Add the juice of an extra lime instead. Only have dried ground ginger? The ginger flavor will be mellow but still tasty. The sauce can even be made with other nut and seed butters. Sunflower butter, in particular, works well and is a great option for those who cannot eat nuts.

YIELD: ABOUT 1¼ CUPS

½ cup smooth, unsweetened peanut butter

1 cup coconut milk (preferably full fat)

1 large handful fresh cilantro with stems intact

2 cloves garlic, smashed

½-inch piece fresh ginger, roughly chopped

2 tablespoons soy sauce or tamari

Zest and juice of 1 lime

1 tablespoon rice vinegar

1 to 2 teaspoons Asian chili sauce, such as sriracha or sambal oelek (adjust for heat tolerance)

1½ tablespoons maple syrup, honey, coconut sugar, or brown sugar

Combine all the ingredients in a food processor or blender and process until smooth.

If the sauce is too thick, add hot water, 1 tablespoon at a time, until the ideal consistency is reached. To make into peanut salad dressing, increase the rice vinegar to 2 tablespoons or add the juice of 1 or 2 more limes.

CASHEW CREMA

This, dairy-free sour cream/Mexican crema dupe is as perfect on tacos (like the Chipotle Carrot Tacos on page 123 or the Yam and Black Bean ones on page 124, Garlic-Crusted Black Bean Quesadillas on page 23, and Kind Veggie Bean and Cheese Burritos on page 18) as it is as the base of a creamy dip. Prepare it as written or swap the vinegar for lemon or lime juice and add chopped fresh herbs like cilantro and parsley for a bit more flavor.

YIELD: ABOUT 1 CUP

- 1 cup raw cashews
- 1 clove garlic
- 2 tablespoons white wine vinegar
- 2 tablespoons neutral oil, such as avocado or grapeseed oil
- ½ teaspoon kosher salt
- ½ teaspoon garlic powder
- ¼ teaspoon onion powder

Put the cashews in a medium bowl, cover with boiling water, and cover with a clean kitchen towel, pot lid, or heat-proof plate for 15 minutes to soften. Drain and rinse the soaked cashews.

Put the cashews and the other ingredients into a blender or food processor and run the machine for 1 to 2 minutes (or longer if necessary) to achieve a very creamy consistency.

Store in an airtight container in the refrigerator for up to a week.

VEGAN GREEN GODDESS DRESSING

Though green goddess dressing was invented in the 1920s (the most widely accepted theory is that it was created by Chef Phillip Roemer, who ran the kitchen at the Palace Hotel in San Francisco, as a tribute to actor George Arliss, then starring in William Archer's play *The Green Goddess*), you might say that the perky, herbaceous green dressing came of age, like many lifelong Dead Heads, in the 1970s.

Unlike the original, however, which was thickened with mayonnaise and got its salty flavor from anchovies, this plant-based rendition relies on raw soaked cashews for creaminess and capers, nutritional yeast, and soy sauce for a fish-free briny punch. Use it to liven up greens, spread it on a sandwich (such as the Mean Green Garlicky Grilled Cheese on page 34), drizzle it over roasted or steamed vegetables, stir it into potato salad, or serve as a dip for bread and crudités.

YIELD: ABOUT 1½ CUPS

¼ cup raw cashews

½ cup loosely packed fresh parsley leaves and stems

½ cup loosely packed fresh cilantro leaves and stems

½ cup packed fresh basil leaves

¼ cup chopped fresh chives or green onions

¼ cup packed fresh tarragon leaves

2 tablespoons water, plus more as needed

1 small clove garlic

1½ teaspoons capers

¼ cup extra-virgin olive oil

2 tablespoons apple cider vinegar

Zest and juice of 1 medium lemon

2 tablespoons nutritional yeast, or more to taste

1 teaspoon soy sauce, tamari, or coconut aminos, or more to taste

Place the cashews in a small bowl and cover with boiling water. Place a lid or a plate over the bowl and let the cashews soak for 15 minutes (alternatively, cover with cold water and let soak overnight).

Place the parsley, cilantro, basil, chives, tarragon, water, garlic, and capers in a blender or food processor. Pulse until finely chopped.

Drain the cashews and add to the herbs in the blender or food processor. Add the olive oil, apple cider vinegar, lemon zest and juice, nutritional yeast, and soy sauce. Process on high speed until smooth. Add more water in 1-tablespoon increments as needed to reach a smooth, pourable consistency. Taste and add more nutritional yeast or a few dashes of soy sauce for additional saltiness if needed.

VEGAN RANCH

Even if you aren't vegan, this ultrarich ranch dressing has a lot going for it, specifically that almost all of its ingredients are shelf-stable pantry staples—no mayo or buttermilk here! Even without the dairy, this fresh take on the classic dressing and dip is still everything you think of when you think of ranch: cool, tangy, creamy, and full of fresh, herby, allium flavor.

YIELD: ABOUT 1½ CUPS

¾ cup raw cashews

⅔ cup water, plus more as needed

½ large or 1 small cucumber, peeled and diced (about ⅔ cup diced)

Juice of 1 medium lemon

1 tablespoon nutritional yeast

½ teaspoon garlic powder

½ teaspoon onion powder

½ teaspoon kosher salt

1 handful fresh dill, finely chopped (about ½ cup chopped), or ½ teaspoon dried dill

2 green onions or 1 small handful fresh chives, cut into 1-inch pieces (2 tablespoons chopped)

Put the cashews in a bowl and cover with boiling water. Cover the bowl with a lid or clean kitchen towel and let sit for 15 minutes to soften. Drain the cashews, then transfer them to a blender or food processor and add the water, cucumber, lemon juice, nutritional yeast, garlic powder, onion powder, salt, dill, and green onions and blend until completely smooth and creamy. Add more water as needed to achieve the desired consistency.

Store the dressing in an airtight jar in the refrigerator for up to a week.

WHOLE LEMON VINAIGRETTE

You've probably made salad dressing with lemon juice before, but this tangy, ever so slightly sweet, bright yellow dressing uses an entire lemon—pith, peel, and fruit—for lemon flavor that will wake you right up. For a naturally sweeter dressing, use a sweeter lemon, like the Meyer variety. The recipe also works with other citrus, such as oranges, tangerines, and even grapefruit (use half a grapefruit, taste, then add more if necessary).

YIELD: ABOUT 1 CUP

1 medium lemon, ends trimmed, seeded, and peel, pith, and fruit roughly chopped

2 tablespoons blanched, toasted almonds

1 shallot, roughly chopped

1 clove garlic, roughly chopped

1 small handful fresh parsley, roughly chopped (about 2 tablespoons chopped)

¾ cup extra-virgin olive oil

2 to 4 teaspoons honey or maple syrup

½ teaspoon kosher salt, or more to taste

A few grinds black pepper

2 tablespoons rice vinegar

Put the lemon, almonds, shallot, garlic, and parsley in a food processor or blender. Pulse until finely chopped. Add the oil, 2 teaspoons of the honey, salt, and pepper, and then stream in the rice vinegar.

Taste and add more honey and salt if necessary. If a thinner consistency is desired, add a bit of water, 1 tablespoon at a time, until the ideal consistency is reached.

Use immediately or store in an airtight container in the refrigerator for up to a week.

MISO-SESAME DRESSING

This is the sort of dressing you'll want to plan your meals around because it's good on everything. Toss it with thinly sliced cabbage (like the Sesame Slaw with Peanuts on page 90) or drizzle over grilled tofu or vegetables and serve with steamed rice or quinoa and toasted sesame seeds for a DIY grain bowl.

YIELD: ABOUT ¾ CUP

2 tablespoons miso paste

1-inch piece fresh ginger, grated

1 large or 2 small cloves garlic, grated or smashed to a paste

1 tablespoon nutritional yeast

1 tablespoon soy sauce or tamari, or more to taste

2 tablespoons toasted sesame oil

¼ cup rice vinegar, or more to taste

¼ cup extra-virgin olive oil, or neutral oil, such as avocado or grapeseed oil

2 tablespoons honey or maple syrup, or more to taste

Combine all the ingredients in a bowl or jar and whisk or shake (covered) well until completely incorporated. Taste and adjust for sweetness (add honey or maple syrup, 1 teaspoon at a time if needed), sharpness (add rice vinegar 1 teaspoon at a time if needed), and saltiness (add a few drops of soy sauce or a little more nutritional yeast until salty enough).

Use immediately or store in an airtight container in the refrigerator for up to a week.

WALNUT-CASHEW PARMESAN

While there are very good vegan Parms on the market, it's easy to make your own. All you need are walnuts, cashews, nutritional yeast, and possibly salt (since nutritional yeast brands can differ in sodium levels, it's important to taste before adding salt; depending on the saltiness of your nutritional yeast, you may not need it).

This Parmesan-esque sprinkle is perfect scattered over the top of a Caesar salad (Green Goddess Caesar with Crispy Tofu Croutons on page 93), stirred into Spring Green Minestrone (page 78), or cascading down a mountain of hot pasta. It's important to note that it does not melt like dairy-based Parmesan cheese. For recipes that call for a melting vegan Parmesan, it's best to opt for a store-bought type, such as the one from Violife.

YIELD: ABOUT ½ CUP

¼ cup raw walnuts

¼ cup raw cashews

1 tablespoon plus 1 teaspoon nutritional yeast

Kosher salt

Put the walnuts, cashews, and nutritional yeast in a food processor. Pulse until the mixture resembles breadcrumbs. (Don't let the machine run for too long, or it will turn into salty nut butter.) Transfer the mixture to a small mixing bowl and taste. If it needs salt, add it ⅛ teaspoon at a time, stirring it into the nut-yeast mixture with a small spoon to fully incorporate, until the desired saltiness is reached.

TOFU PESTO

Between the hefty ¾ cup pine nuts or walnuts and the firm or extra-firm tofu that stands in for the usual Parmesan, this vibrant green, lemony sauce boasts an impressive 8 grams of protein per ¼-cup serving. Certainly you could toss it with hot or cold pasta, but it's also wonderful as a dip or sandwich spread, stirred into rice, or in place of the usual marinara sauce in lasagna.

Replacing half the basil with green onions and artichoke hearts yields different but equally good results. For cilantro pesto, replace the basil with cilantro leaves and stems, and use almonds or sunflower seeds in place of the pine nuts and/or walnuts. You can even substitute beet greens or carrot tops for half the basil and toss the pesto with vegetables for the ultimate no-waste veggie dish.

YIELD: ABOUT 2 CUPS

3 cups fresh basil leaves and stems, tightly packed

¾ cup pine nuts or chopped walnuts (or a combination)

2 medium cloves garlic, smashed

8 ounces firm or extra-firm tofu

¼ cup extra-virgin olive oil

Zest and juice of 1 medium lemon

1 teaspoon kosher salt, or more to taste

In a food processor, pulse the basil, pine nuts, and garlic until finely chopped. Crumble the tofu and add to the food processor. Pulse a few times to combine.

Scrape the basil-nut-tofu mixture into a medium bowl and stir in the olive oil, lemon zest and juice, and salt. The pesto may be used right away, but it will taste better after at least an hour in the refrigerator to allow the flavors to meld.

OPENING ACT

STARTERS AND SNACKS

Smaller Dead shows might not feature an opener, but bigger stadiums might begin the night with another act. Imagine standing in the pit, waiting for the show to start, seeing the lights come up, then hearing opening chords. And that's before the show you came to see begins! Talk about a miracle.

This approach to minimalism/maximalism is good advice when it comes to cooking and entertaining. If you think of the entirety of a meal as a show, then your dinner table is the venue. When the show is smaller and less elaborate—when you're expecting fewer people or it's a low-key event—it makes sense to scale back and serve a simpler meal. You prepare an entrée, maybe bake some bread, throw together a salad, and serve a homemade dessert, like cookies or some fine ice cream. For the right occasion, that's the definition of a perfect meal.

When the crowd is bigger, the event is especially festive, and you're celebrating, it's a fun time to go all out. That means more food—maybe a few entrées, multiple sides, and desserts. To kick things off, offer your own opening act using the recipes in this chapter for little bites, snacks, and appetizers to get everyone warmed up for the good time that lies ahead.

BUFFALO TOFU

If you've ever felt left out watching your friends chow down on buffalo wings, licking the bright-red sauce off their fingers while you glumly crunch on the celery and carrot sticks (which everyone knows are basically just a garnish), then this recipe is for you. Here, ever the chameleon, tofu is lightly fried until crispy, then tossed in a spicy, buttery buffalo sauce (which is just as good prepared with plant-based butter as it is with the real stuff). Serve on a plate with a creamy dressing (like Vegan Ranch on page 48), along with carrots and/or celery sticks. Whether you choose to share with your chicken-loving friends or not is up to you.

YIELD: 6-8 SERVINGS

1 cup cayenne-based hot sauce, such as Crystal or Tabasco

2 tablespoons white vinegar

¼ cup packed brown sugar

½ cup (1 stick) unsalted butter (dairy or plant based)

½ teaspoon chili powder

¼ teaspoon salt, or more to taste

2 cloves garlic, minced

3 tablespoons neutral oil, such as avocado or grapeseed oil, plus more as needed for frying

Two 16-ounce blocks extra-firm tofu, drained, patted dry, and cut into 1½-by-½-inch pieces

In a medium pot over medium-high heat, whisk together the hot sauce, white vinegar, brown sugar, butter, chili powder, salt, and garlic. Stir well to combine.

Let the sauce come to a light boil, then reduce the heat to medium and let cook for 10 to 12 minutes, until thickened. While the sauce cooks, heat the oil in a large frying pan over medium-high heat.

Working in batches, fry the tofu pieces for 2 or 3 minutes on one side, until a thick, golden crust develops. Flip the tofu pieces and cook for another 2 to 3 minutes on the other side. The tofu should be quite crisp.

Pour the thickened buffalo sauce into the frying pan and swirl it around to coat the tofu pieces evenly. Cook for 5 to 7 minutes, turning the tofu pieces a few times during cooking to ensure an even coating of the sauce. Use tongs or a spatula to carefully transfer the cooked tofu to a serving plate.

CHICKPEA-KALE SPANAKOPITA TRIANGLES

Spanakopita means "spinach pie" in Greek, so it's fair to say these crisp mini pies, which are made with kale instead of the traditional spinach, are perhaps a little bit liberally named. Even so, they have a lot going for them. First, these tasty little pastry pockets could just as easily be called pocket pastries, depending on where and how you eat them (on a picnic blanket with good people, a cold drink, and live music is an ideal place to start), thanks to their easy portability (once cool, they'll hold up for hours without getting soggy). Better yet, in each crispy little phyllo-wrapped, sesame seed–topped triangle, you'll find earthy kale (if you're a real stickler for tradition, you could opt for spinach), creamy feta (vegan feta and/or crumbled firm tofu works nicely), ricotta, fresh herbs, crunchy red bell peppers, and chickpeas.

YIELD: 25 TRIANGLES

FOR THE FILLING

One 16-ounce bag frozen kale

½ cup extra-virgin olive oil

10 green onions, finely chopped

4 cloves garlic, finely chopped

½ teaspoon kosher salt, or more to taste (the saltiness of your feta will determine whether you need more; see the instructions)

3 or 4 grinds fresh black pepper

1 large handful fresh parsley, chopped (about ½ cup chopped)

1 large handful fresh dill, chopped (about ½ cup chopped)

6 ounces feta cheese, crumbled (substitute vegan feta or crumbled firm tofu for a vegan version)

6 ounces ricotta or cottage cheese (substitute store-bought vegan ricotta, like the almond-based one from Kite Hill)

½ large red bell pepper, seeded and finely chopped (about ½ cup chopped)

1 cup chickpeas (about half of one 15-ounce can), drained and rinsed

Zest of 1 medium lemon

½ teaspoon red pepper flakes, or more to taste

2 large eggs (or substitute egg replacer or flax eggs; see Note on page 12)

To make the filling: Thaw the kale by letting it sit overnight in the refrigerator or by emptying it into a microwave-safe bowl and microwaving on high power for 1½ to 2 minutes. Transfer the thawed kale to a clean kitchen towel and twist tightly to squeeze as much moisture out as possible.

Heat 1 tablespoon of the olive oil in a large frying pan over medium-high heat and cook the green onions until soft and fragrant, 2 to 3 minutes.

In a large mixing bowl, combine the kale, cooked green onions, and the rest of the filling ingredients except the eggs. Mix well and taste. If it needs more salt, add it in ¼-teaspoon increments until the desired saltiness is reached. Once you're happy with the flavor, add the eggs and mix well.

Preheat the oven to 350°F and position a rack in the middle of the oven. Grease two rimmed baking sheets or line them with parchment paper or a silicone baking mat.

CONTINUES

FOR ASSEMBLY

25 sheets phyllo pastry, thawed if frozen

⅓ cup olive oil, plus more as needed

2 tablespoons untoasted sesame seeds (white, black, or a mixture)

To assemble the triangles: Use a sharp knife to cut through the phyllo vertically so you have 50 long strips. Put any leftover phyllo away so it doesn't dry out. Lay a strip of phyllo on a clean, dry workspace. Brush liberally with olive oil, then top with a second strip. Place a heaping tablespoon of the filling at the end of the strip. Fold the end of your strip with the filling over to encase the filling and form a triangle. Brush the rest of the strip of phyllo with olive oil.

Continue tightly folding the triangle until you get to the end and have a neat triangle. Tuck any spare ends underneath the pastry and place the completed pie on the prepared baking sheet. Brush with oil and sprinkle with sesame seeds. (Omit this step for any triangles you don't want to bake immediately. Freeze them on the baking sheet, then transfer to an airtight container to remain in the freezer and save this step for when you want to bake them from frozen.)

Repeat until the rest of the pies are assembled, dividing them between the two prepared baking sheets so as not to overcrowd them.

Working in batches, bake for 18 to 22 minutes, or until golden brown. Transfer to a wire rack to cool and serve warm or at room temperature.

CRISPY SPICED CHICKPEAS

Is there nothing the humble chickpea cannot do? From hummus to curry to veggie burgers, it is highly versatile for a humble legume. Here, ultracheap canned chickpeas give chips, crackers, and roasted nuts a run for their money in the crispy party snack category. They need only a little oil, salt, spices, and a longish time in a lowish oven. Don't be tempted to crank up the heat: These babies need time to achieve ultimate crunch.

YIELD: ABOUT 1½ CUPS

Two 15-ounce cans chickpeas, drained, rinsed, and dried completely with a clean kitchen towel

2 tablespoons neutral oil, such as avocado or grapeseed oil

1 teaspoon kosher salt

1 teaspoon smoked paprika

¼ teaspoon ground cumin

½ teaspoon garlic powder

½ teaspoon onion powder

Preheat the oven to 350°F.

Put the chickpeas in a large mixing bowl and add the oil. Stir well to coat. Then add the salt and stir again. Divide the chickpeas between two ungreased rimmed baking sheets, then bake for 15 minutes and switch the pans: Put the lower one on the upper rack and the upper one on the lower rack. Bake for another 15 minutes.

While the chickpeas bake, mix the paprika, cumin, garlic powder, and onion powder in a small bowl. Remove the pans from the oven and combine onto one baking sheet: The chickpeas will have shrunk quite a bit, so they'll all fit nicely. Sprinkle half the spices over the chickpeas. Use a spatula to mix them well to make sure they're all nicely coated.

Return the pan to the oven and place on the upper rack for 10 to 15 minutes. The chickpeas should be browned but not burned and very crispy. Let the chickpeas cool completely on the baking sheet, a step that helps crisp them further. They'll be a little soft right out of the oven, so don't skip the cooling.

Once completely cool, toss the roasted chickpeas with the remaining spices. Serve these on the day you make them. They do not improve with time.

BAKED SAMOSAS WITH MINTY PEACH CHUTNEY

Like the Spanakopita Triangles on page 59, these crispy little packages may not look like much, but one bite—especially dipped in the fruity, minty chutney—and you will realize these are far more than meets the eye. Though these are not exactly traditional (samosas are usually made with a rich wheat-based wrapper, studded with ajwain, also known as carom, a tiny seed-like fruit, and then fried until golden), this lighter, easier alternative is still heavily influenced by the real deal. Although the recipe calls for the samosas to be baked, you can, of course, fry them—either in a deep fryer or in a few inches of oil in a heavy-bottomed pot. They also crisp up quite nicely in an air fryer. If you choose to air-fry, start by cooking them for 10 minutes, then cook for a few minutes longer if necessary to get them nicely browned and bubbly skinned.

YIELD: 15 SAMOSAS

FOR THE SAMOSAS

1½ teaspoons kosher salt, or more to taste

4 medium or 3 large russet potatoes, peeled and cut into quarters

1 tablespoon neutral oil, such as avocado or grapeseed oil, or ghee (clarified butter), plus more for the pan and for brushing

1 white onion, diced

½-inch piece fresh ginger, minced or grated

1½ teaspoons garam masala

½ teaspoon ground coriander

¼ teaspoon ground cumin

2 cloves garlic, minced

½ cup frozen green peas

15 large wrappers (wrapper sizes vary between brands, but you're looking for something 6½ to 8 inches square)

Preheat the oven to 425°F and arrange a rack in the center of the oven. Lightly grease (or line with parchment paper or a silicone baking mat) a baking sheet and set aside.

To make the samosas: Bring a medium pot of water to a boil over high heat and add 1 teaspoon of the salt. Reduce the heat to medium and add the potatoes. Cook for 12 to 14 minutes, until very soft. Drain and cool the cooked potatoes in a large bowl.

Heat the oil in a large frying pan over medium heat. Add the onion and cook for 2 to 3 minutes, until it is soft and fragrant. Add the ginger, spices, and remaining ½ teaspoon salt, stirring to mix completely. Cook for 30 seconds to 1 minute, until very fragrant; be careful not to let the spices burn. Remove from the heat and transfer to the bowl with the potatoes.

Add the garlic and peas to the potato mixture and mix vigorously with a wooden spoon, a fork, or your hands, ensuring the spice mixture seasons the potatoes thoroughly. Take it easy, though—you are not making mashed potatoes. There should be lots of lumps. Taste for seasoning and add more salt if necessary.

Stack the wrappers on top of each other and use a sharp knife to cut across them diagonally so each wrapper consists of two large triangles. Wet one of the shorter edges of each triangle, using your finger or a pastry brush, and lay it on top of the other short edge to create a long cone. Put 1½ to 2 heaping tablespoons of filling in the center of the wrapper (depending on how much you can fit without it bursting). Fold in the top flaps and use a little water to seal. Repeat until all the wrappers and filling are used. Transfer the samosas to the prepared baking sheet. You may have to work in batches.

FOR THE CHUTNEY

1 medium white or yellow peach (it should be very ripe), peeled, pitted, and coarsely chopped (if you can't find ripe peaches, 1 cup thawed frozen peeled peaches or 1 cup chopped fresh or frozen mango works well as substitutes)

1 medium shallot or ¼ medium red onion, roughly chopped

½ cup tightly packed fresh mint leaves

½ cup tightly packed fresh cilantro leaves

⅛ teaspoon ground cumin

⅛ teaspoon ground cardamom

1-inch piece fresh ginger, chopped

½ cup plain yogurt (dairy or plant based)

1 to 2 teaspoons maple syrup or honey, as needed

¼ teaspoon kosher salt, or more to taste

Brush the samosas lightly with oil, coating the wrappers evenly. Bake for 20 to 24 minutes, or until the samosas are golden brown and slightly bubbly.

To make the chutney: Combine all the ingredients in a blender and pulse until mostly smooth (a few chunks are nice). Taste, and if you'd like it to be sweeter, add a bit of maple syrup or honey, 1 teaspoon at a time.

Serve the samosas hot with the sauce alongside for dipping.

NOTE: If preferred, these may be served with Leafy Green Relish (page 38).

CARROT-LENTIL HUMMUS

Purists might balk at the use of *hummus* in the title of this recipe, but once they taste it, ideally on warm bread or with a spoonful of Spicy-Crunchy Chili Oil (page 40) drizzled on for good measure, they'll find it impossible to care. Roasting the carrots turns them sweet and gives them a deep caramelized flavor that works beautifully with mild, quick-cooking red lentils (the hummus may be prepared with other types of lentils or even chickpeas, but make sure they are thoroughly cooked, almost to the point of falling apart). Serve with warm bread and/or sliced vegetables.

YIELD: 6–8 SERVINGS

- 4 medium carrots, ends trimmed and cut into 2-inch pieces (no need to peel)
- 1 medium yellow onion, quartered
- 3 cloves garlic, ends trimmed
- 5 tablespoons extra-virgin olive oil, plus more for garnish
- 1 teaspoon kosher salt
- A few grinds black pepper
- ½ teaspoon curry powder
- 1 teaspoon smoked paprika
- ½ cup uncooked red lentils, thoroughly rinsed
- ¼ cup fresh cilantro leaves, plus more for garnish (optional)
- ¼ cup tahini
- Zest and juice of 1 medium lemon
- ½ teaspoon ground cumin
- ½ teaspoon ground coriander
- ½ teaspoon sumac, plus more for garnish

Preheat the oven to 400°F.

Place the carrots, onion, and two cloves of the garlic on a rimmed baking sheet. Drizzle with 2 tablespoons of the olive oil and sprinkle with ½ teaspoon of the salt, pepper, curry powder, and smoked paprika. Toss the vegetables well to coat and spread them out on the baking sheet.

Roast the carrots and onion for 20 to 25 minutes, or until tender and lightly browned, tossing halfway through baking.

Meanwhile, combine the lentils and enough water to cover in a medium saucepan over high heat. Bring to a boil, reduce the heat to medium, and cook uncovered for 10 to 15 minutes, or until the lentils are soft. Reserve ½ cup cooking of the liquid, then drain.

Transfer the roasted carrots, onion, remaining 3 tablespoons olive oil, and cooked lentils to a food processor or blender, along with the cilantro, tahini, lemon zest and juice, remaining ½ teaspoon salt, remaining 1 clove garlic, cumin, coriander, and sumac. Pulse until mostly smooth, scraping down the sides as needed. If the hummus is too thick, thin it with a bit of the reserved lentil cooking liquid, adding 1 tablespoon at a time.

Taste and season with more salt if desired. Scrape the hummus into a serving bowl, drizzle with more olive oil, and garnish with cilantro leaves if desired and a light sprinkle of sumac.

NOTE: If you can't find sumac, substitute cayenne pepper or a bit of freshly ground black pepper. It won't be exactly the same, but it will still be quite good.

CLASSIC HUMMUS

If you think of hummus as something that comes in a plastic tub, then your mind is about to be changed forever. Though the ingredients in this recipe are simple and cheap, the results are smooth, creamy, bursting with bright flavor, and ethereally light. One taste of the homemade stuff and you'll never want to touch the store-bought variety again. Serve this with chips, veggies, or warm bread. Leftovers will keep in an airtight container in the refrigerator for up to a week.

YIELD: 8–10 SERVINGS

- 2 cups dried chickpeas
- 3 tablespoons baking soda
- ¼ cup extra-virgin olive oil, plus more for garnish
- ¼ cup tahini
- ⅛ teaspoon ground cumin
- Juice of 1 lemon
- 2 cloves garlic, roughly chopped
- 1 teaspoon kosher salt, or more to taste

Pick over the dried chickpeas and remove any that are still green. Put the chickpeas in a large, heavy-bottomed pot and add enough water to cover the chickpeas by about 2 inches.

Stir in the baking soda. Cover the pot and bring to a boil over high heat. Reduce the heat to medium and simmer for 5 minutes. Let the chickpeas sit in the pot, covered, for 10 minutes.

Turn off the heat, reserve ½ cup of the chickpea cooking liquid, and drain the chickpeas using a colander or strainer. Run cold water over the chickpeas until they are cool to the touch.

Working in small batches, rub a handful of chickpeas between your hands to remove the peels. Repeat until most of the peels have been removed from the chickpeas. Place the peeled chickpeas back in the pot and cover with 2 to 3 inches of water. Cover the pot with the lid.

Bring to a boil, then reduce the heat to medium-low. Simmer for 1 hour 15 minutes and then lift the lid and use a slotted spoon to remove any peels that have floated to the top during cooking.

Drain the chickpeas in a colander or strainer and run cold water over them to bring them to room temperature. Place the chickpeas in a food processor. Run the machine until all lumps disappear and the chickpeas are very smooth. With the machine running, stream in the olive oil.

Add the tahini, cumin, lemon juice, garlic, and salt and blend until the hummus is completely smooth.

Scrape the hummus into a serving bowl and garnish with a drizzle of olive oil and/or any herbs, spices, or other garnishes you like (such as za'atar, sumac, fresh parsley, or even toasted sesame seeds).

CASHEW CARAMELIZED ONION DIP

This onion dip is everything you want in party food: ultracreamy and stacked with three different layers of allium flavor—deeply caramelized, milder, and garlic and onion powders and a pop of green freshness from green onions or chives. Unlike the onion dip you make from a packet, however, this recipe lacks even a trace of sour cream. Rather, this vegan-friendly take on onion dip is made creamy with silken tofu. Make sure to use the silken variety; regular tofu won't turn creamy in quite the same way when blended. In addition to making it a good option for animal-free eaters, the tofu adds a hefty boost of protein without adding the fat and cholesterol that sour cream does. Try it as a dip for fries (like the Crispy Sweet Potato Oven Fries on page 103), chips, bread, vegetables, crackers, or anything else that would taste good dragged through a creamy, savory dip. It may also be thinned with a bit of rice vinegar or apple cider vinegar and used as a salad dressing or spread on sandwiches for a rich and creamy aioli alternative.

YIELD: 6–8 SERVINGS

3 tablespoons neutral oil, such as avocado or grapeseed oil

2 medium yellow onions, thinly sliced

1 teaspoon kosher salt, or more to taste

1 teaspoon soy sauce, tamari, or coconut aminos

2 tablespoons rice vinegar or apple cider vinegar, or more to taste

¼ cup white wine or water

One 12-ounce package soft silken tofu

2 tablespoons nutritional yeast

½ teaspoon garlic powder

½ teaspoon onion powder

¼ teaspoon freshly ground black pepper, or more to taste

2 green onions, green parts only, or 1 small bundle fresh chives, roughly chopped

Heat the oil in a large frying pan over medium heat. Add the onions and stir well to coat with the oil, then reduce the heat to medium-low. Cook for 25 to 30 minutes, stirring occasionally (reduce the heat to low if the onions start to sizzle), until browned and very soft.

In a small bowl, whisk together the salt, soy sauce, vinegar, and wine. Pour over the onions to deglaze the pan, using a wooden spoon to scrape up any browned bits, and stirring them into the onions and liquid. Continue to cook for about 5 minutes, until the liquid cooks down and the onions are deeply browned.

Put the tofu into a food processor and add the nutritional yeast, garlic powder, onion powder, salt, and pepper. Pulse a few times until creamy and smooth. Add the caramelized onion mixture and green onions and pulse a few times to combine (you're not looking for a completely smooth dip). Taste and adjust as needed, adding more salt and/or vinegar.

VEGETABLE SUMMER ROLLS

These all-veggie rolls are wrapped tightly in a chewy rice noodle wrapper and meant to be dipped in a flavorful sauce, such as Peanut Sauce (page 45), bottled Thai sweet chili sauce, or salty-sweet hoisin. Think of the fillings listed here as mere suggestions, as these are good with just about any vegetable, making them an ideal dish to update with the seasons. Try roasted sweet potato or kabocha squash and spinach in autumn, pea shoots and ramps in spring, thinly sliced apples and roasted leeks in winter, and grilled eggplant and sweet corn in summer. Serve the rolls sliced on the bias with your preferred dipping sauce.

YIELD: 10 ROLLS

Ten 8-inch rice paper spring roll wrappers

20 fresh mint leaves

1 red bell pepper, seeded and cut into matchsticks

2 carrots, peeled and shredded

½ cucumber, peeled, seeded, and cut into matchsticks

2 green onions, cut into thin 2-inch strips

Wet a spring roll wrapper under the tap or in a bowl of room-temperature water and shake gently to remove excess liquid. Place the wrapper on a clean, dry surface. Arrange 2 mint leaves in the center of the wrapper. Lay 2 or 3 pieces of bell pepper, a generous pinch of shredded carrots, a few pieces of cucumber, and 1 or 2 slices of green onion on top of the mint, making sure that all ingredients are facing in the same direction. Once the wrapper is pliable enough to work with, tuck in the ends and roll up tightly, like a little burrito. Don't worry if you mess a few up; this takes practice. Repeat until all the ingredients are used.

TOFU SUSHI ROLLS

Restaurant sushi, even the vegetarian kind, can get expensive, but these tofu-and-veggie rolls are as cost-effective as they are tasty. Even better, they're a lot of fun to make with friends. Put on your favorite Dead album, open a few icy beers, a bottle of sake, or sparkling apple cider, and invite your crew into the kitchen for some sushi-rolling fun. If you want to switch things up a little, try brown sushi rice instead of the white, substitute any thinly sliced vegetables or fresh greens you prefer for the mixed greens, or use tempeh instead of the tofu or leave it out altogether and just use more cooked or raw vegetables in its place.

YIELD: 30 PIECES

2 tablespoons soy sauce, tamari, or coconut aminos, plus more for dipping

2 tablespoons neutral oil, such as avocado or grapeseed oil, plus more for the baking sheet

2 tablespoons honey or maple syrup

1-inch piece fresh ginger, minced

2 cloves garlic, minced

8 ounces firm or extra-firm tofu, drained, patted dry, and cut into 3-inch strips

1 cup white sushi rice

2 teaspoons rice vinegar

6 sheets roasted sushi nori

2 cups mixed greens

3 green onions, cut lengthwise and then into 3-inch strips

Wasabi paste and pickled ginger, for serving

In a medium bowl, whisk together the soy sauce, oil, honey, ginger, and garlic. Place the sliced tofu in the bowl and use your hands to ensure each piece of tofu is coated. Let marinate for at least 30 minutes and up to 12 hours.

When the tofu has finished marinating, preheat the oven to 375°F. Lightly oil a baking sheet or line it with parchment paper or a silicone baking mat.

Spread the marinated tofu on the prepared baking sheet and bake for 18 to 20 minutes, flipping the pieces halfway through. Remove and let cool for 5 to 10 minutes.

While the tofu bakes, cook the rice according to the package instructions. Spread it on a plate to cool and, once cool to room temperature, sprinkle with the rice vinegar. Set aside.

To assemble the sushi rolls, lay a piece of nori on a clean, dry surface lengthwise and shiny side down. Wet your hands with cool water and spread one-sixth of the rice over the bottom half of the nori sheet. Arrange one-sixth of the mixed greens evenly over the rice. Lay a few strips of tofu in a row on top of the greens. Place a few pieces of green onion along the tofu.

Roll up the nori sheet tightly, starting at the bottom. Use a finger dipped in water to seal the end of the nori to the rest of the roll. Cut into five pieces (using a very sharp or serrated knife helps). Repeat with the remaining ingredients.

Serve immediately with more soy sauce, wasabi paste, and pickled ginger.

LENTIL NACHOS

If you feel strongly that lentils don't belong on nachos, feel free to use black beans, pintos, or whatever beans you choose, but if you're willing to be a little open-minded about it, this recipe will surely convert you. Lentils beautifully absorb the flavors of the spices added to them, and because they are so petite, you get to drag more of that gorgeous flavor into your mouth with every bite because, unlike larger beans, they do a better job of staying attached to the chips and cheese.

YIELD: 4–6 SERVINGS

2 cups cooked green or brown lentils

⅛ teaspoon ground cumin

¼ teaspoon chili powder

¼ teaspoon garlic powder

¼ teaspoon kosher salt

6 cups tortilla chips

8 ounces cheddar or jack cheese, shredded (or 2 cups Better Cheddar Vegan Cheese Dip on page 74 or store-bought vegan cheese shreds, slices, or dip)

1 green jalapeño, seeded and sliced, or one 4-ounce can chopped green chiles

2 ripe avocados, peeled, halved, pitted, and diced

¼ small red onion, diced, or ½ cup Quick-Pickled Onions (page 41), roughly chopped

2 small tomatoes, cored and diced, or 1 cup cherry tomatoes, halved

1 large handful fresh cilantro, chopped (about 1/2 cup chopped)

½ cup dairy or plant-based sour cream or Greek yogurt (optional)

Store-bought salsa or hot sauce, for garnish

Preheat the oven to 375°F.

In a medium bowl, stir the lentils together with the cumin, chili powder, garlic powder, and salt to combine. Spread the chips over an ungreased rimmed baking sheet. Scatter the seasoned lentils over the chips. Cover with the cheese and bake for 10 to 12 minutes, or until the cheese has melted and is bubbly.

Top the baked nachos with the jalapeño, avocados, onion, tomatoes, cilantro, and sour cream, if using. Dot with salsa.

Serve immediately; the nachos do not improve with time, so it's best to eat them when the chips are crisp and the cheese is hot and melty.

MAGIC STUFFED MUSHROOMS

The magic of these stuffed mushrooms is that by combining just a few simple ingredients and easy techniques, it's possible to turn regular old supermarket button mushrooms into something truly out of this world. Simultaneously earthy and fresh tasting, juicy and crisp, buttery yet free of any butter, they're a contradiction of the tastiest sort. They're perfect as a passed appetizer, but also very good over a bed of greens. Substitute gluten-free breadcrumbs for the panko for a gluten-free version.

YIELD: 15 STUFFED MUSHROOMS

15 medium button mushrooms

3 tablespoons extra-virgin olive oil

½ teaspoon kosher salt

½ cup grated Parmesan (dairy or plant based)

⅓ cup panko breadcrumbs

2 cloves garlic, minced

1 large handful fresh parsley, finely chopped (about 2 tablespoons chopped)

A few grinds black pepper

Preheat the oven to 400°F and lightly grease (or line with parchment paper or a silicone baking mat) a rimmed baking sheet.

Gently remove the stems from the mushroom caps and set aside. Use a pastry brush to lightly brush the mushroom caps with 1½ tablespoons of the olive oil. Arrange the mushrooms on the baking sheet, cavity side up, and lightly sprinkle with ¼ teaspoon of the salt.

In a bowl, combine the Parmesan, breadcrumbs, garlic, parsley, remaining ¼ teaspoon salt, pepper, and remaining 1½ tablespoons olive oil. Stir thoroughly to combine. Stuff each mushroom with 2 heaping teaspoons of the filling.

Bake for 20 to 22 minutes, or until the mushrooms are very tender and the filling has browned nicely. Serve hot or at room temperature.

BETTER CHEDDAR VEGAN CHEESE DIP

There are many good plant-based cheeses on the market, but they're not without drawbacks. Many contain stabilizers that some people don't digest well, and most of them are pricey. So what do you do when you don't eat (or are trying to cut back on) dairy, and the craving for a Grateful Dead preshow Garlicky Grilled Cheese (page 30) or a Kind Veggie Bean and Cheese Burrito (page 18) hits? Easy! Make a vegan cheese that can do it all. This cheddar-like dip is creamy, savory, and gooey, just like the real thing. Its unctuousness comes from pan-toasted cashews, which deepens their flavor, cooked slowly in water, which helps them turn ultracreamy when blended with liquid, carrots, and potatoes. Its cheesy tang comes from nutritional yeast, plus a little mustard and hot sauce.

The cheese sauce may be served immediately, over chips for nachos, fresh bread or vegetables for fondue, or any other way you'd use melted cheese. Alternatively, allow it to cool and thicken slightly and use as a spread on everything from crackers and bread to grilled cheese sandwiches.

YIELD: 6–8 SERVINGS

¼ cup neutral oil, such as avocado or grapeseed oil

1 small onion, thinly sliced

2 cloves garlic, roughly chopped

½ teaspoon salt, plus or more to taste

½ teaspoon ground cumin

1 teaspoon smoked paprika

1 teaspoon garlic powder

½ medium russet potato, peeled and chopped (about ½ cup chopped)

1 medium carrot, peeled and chopped

¾ cup raw cashews

2 cups water

½ cup unsweetened almond, soy, or other plant-based milk

1 teaspoon hot sauce, or more to taste (optional)

3 tablespoons nutritional yeast

1 teaspoon prepared smooth mustard (like Dijon or yellow mustard, not whole-grain mustard)

2½ teaspoons white distilled or rice vinegar

Heat the oil in a medium frying pan over medium heat. Add the onion and garlic and cook, stirring, for 3 to 4 minutes, until very soft and translucent. Add the salt, cumin, smoked paprika, and garlic powder. Cook, stirring, for about 1 minute, until the mixture is fragrant and starts to sizzle.

Add the potato, carrot, and cashews and cook, stirring frequently, just until the cashews begin to brown, about 2 minutes. Add the water and milk. Raise the heat to high, bring to a boil, and cover the pan. Reduce the heat to low and simmer with the lid on for 8 to 10 minutes, stirring frequently, until the potatoes and carrots are very soft.

Carefully pour the mixture into a blender or food processor. Add the hot sauce, if using, nutritional yeast, mustard, 2 teaspoons of the vinegar and blend on low speed, adding 1 or 2 tablespoons more water if necessary to help the mixture blend smoothly. Process on high speed until completely smooth. Add more water as needed if the mixture becomes too thick. Taste and adjust the seasonings as needed: a pinch of salt, ½ teaspoon more vinegar, or more hot sauce, for example.

BAKED JALAPEÑO POPPERS

Jalapeño poppers are always a crowd-pleaser; rarely has it taken more than 10 minutes for a platter of them to be devoured. But making the deep-fried kind can be a messy hassle that leaves you with a grease-splattered kitchen, a pot full of capsaicin-tainted hot oil, and a lot of dishes. This easier, cleaner approach to the classic app has a lot of benefits. First, because the jalapeños are sliced lengthwise, filled, and baked open-faced (rather than skewered back together and fried, per the traditional recipe), you're able to get two poppers for every one pepper. Second, filling and baking takes you from cooking in the kitchen to enjoying spicy, cheesy deliciousness a whole lot faster, and finally—perhaps most important—they come with a bonus chef's treat that is almost more delicious than the poppers themselves: little bits of crispy cheese filling that spill out of the blistered peppers and onto the baking sheet.

YIELD: 20 POPPERS

- One 8-ounce package cream cheese, at room temperature
- 4 ounces jack or cheddar cheese, grated
- 1 clove garlic, finely minced
- 1 teaspoon chili powder
- ¼ teaspoon ground cumin
- ½ teaspoon smoked paprika
- ¼ teaspoon kosher salt
- ¼ teaspoon freshly ground black pepper
- 10 green jalapeños, sliced in half lengthwise, seeds and veins scraped out
- 2 tablespoons unsalted butter (dairy or plant based), melted
- ¼ cup grated Parmesan cheese

Preheat the oven to 350°F.

In a medium mixing bowl, combine the cream cheese and jack cheese, garlic, spices, salt, and pepper. Stir well to combine.

Use a spoon to pack each jalapeño half with 1 to 1½ tablespoons of the mixture. If you have leftover filling, save it to spread on crackers, fill omelets, or use in place of cheese in a grilled cheese sandwich. Arrange the poppers, filled side up, on an ungreased baking sheet, sprinkle each with a pinch of Parmesan, and bake for 20 to 24 minutes, or until the peppers are softened, the cheese is melted, and the tops are lightly browned.

If, after baking, you want the tops browned further, pop them under the broiler for a minute or two. Let cool for at least 5 minutes. Serve warm.

NOTE: For vegan poppers, substitute 1½ cups Better Cheddar Vegan Cheese Dip (page 74) for the cream cheese and grated cheese.

TUNING UP

SOUPS AND SALADS

If you've ever been to a Dead show, you know how exciting it is to listen to the band tune their instruments before beginning to play.

Grateful Dead tune-up sessions turn a necessary preshow step into a lot of fun for everyone. They are one-part guessing game, one-part teaser, and one-part lively conversation between the Dead and Dead Heads. As eager concertgoers await the start of the show, the band members adjust their sound levels, twist their tuning pegs, and pluck their guitar strings, seemingly unfocused on the crowd. An on-key chord might play followed by a tap-tap-tap of the drums and a few low strums on the bass. *Ah!* you might think to yourself. *The show is about to start!* A familiar tune fills the air, and fans wonder if it's go-time. But after a few notes, it becomes clear that it isn't a Dead song they were playing, or even that of another band. Rather, a classic nursery rhyme—"Itsy Bitsy Spider," perhaps, or "Little Bunny Foo Foo." Just a little joke between the band and their loving fans.

After another few minutes of tuning, a clear, cohesive, and familiar sound might blast from the stage, and this time it's even more exciting because the fans recognize it as a Dead song. Then, a couple of opening notes or even a few chords of one of their songs fill the air—a signal to the audience that it'll be on the night's set list—a little amuse-bouche of what showgoers can expect.

When you're putting together a meal, soups and salads serve a similar purpose. Generally, they're served in quantities that aren't quite substantial enough to constitute a full meal but are just enough to whet a diner's appetite and set the tone for the food to come.

Of course, this is not to say you can't make a full meal of these soups and salads. Ladle or plate a large portion, add some warm bread, maybe a drizzle of a special condiment or two, and you're in business.

SPRING GREEN MINESTRONE

This bright yet savory soup is a celebration of all things fresh, green, and vibrant. Make it on the cusp of spring to usher in the season ahead, as the icy chill begins to retreat, the sun starts showing its face again, and the warm-weather veggies in this soup—zucchini, asparagus, spring peas, tender baby spinach—start making appearances at your local farmers' market. Or make it in the dead of winter, when you find yourself in need of something to brighten the long, dark days, using the best quality frozen veggies you can source. It may not be quite the same as when you make it with the fresh stuff, but it will still be delicious, and, just like listening to a recorded Dead show, it'll help you conjure a bit of that bliss you're longing for. This recipe is dedicated to Steve Silberman, a huge Dead Head, writer, and soup connoisseur who passed away in 2024.

YIELD: 4 SERVINGS

3 tablespoons extra-virgin olive oil

1 yellow onion, diced

4 cloves garlic, minced

1 tablespoon nutritional yeast

1 teaspoon kosher salt, or more to taste

3 cups vegetable broth or prepared vegetable bouillon

3 cups water

2 cups small pasta, such as shells, macaroni elbows, or fusilli

One 14-ounce can Great Northern white beans, cannellini beans, white navy beans, or chickpeas, drained and rinsed

8 ounces asparagus, ends trimmed and cut into 1-inch pieces

1 medium zucchini, diced

½ cup fresh or frozen baby peas

3 packed cups baby spinach

4 tablespoons Tofu Pesto (page 53) or store-bought basil pesto

Grated Parmesan cheese, store-bought vegan Parmesan, or Walnut-Cashew Parmesan (page 52)

Heat a large pot (at least 6 quarts) over medium heat and add the olive oil and onion and cook, stirring often, just until fragrant, 2 to 3 minutes. Add the garlic, nutritional yeast, and salt, stirring well to disperse the seasonings, and cook for another minute, until the onion begins to brown.

Add the broth and water. Cover the pot and turn the heat up to high to bring to a boil. Reduce the heat to medium-low and simmer for 12 minutes. Taste the soup and add more salt if needed.

Raise the heat to medium-high and bring to a boil. Add the pasta and cook for 5 to 6 minutes. For a thicker short pasta like fusilli or gemelli, check the cooking instructions on the package and reduce the cooking time by 2 to 3 minutes. The pasta should be al dente at this point.

Add the white beans, asparagus, and zucchini. Cover and cook for another 2 to 3 minutes, until the asparagus has softened a bit (you may need less time if your asparagus is very thin). Add the peas and spinach, then stir well. Taste the soup one more time, adding salt if necessary.

Ladle the soup into bowls, stir 1 tablespoon of the pesto into each one, then top generously with the Parmesan.

KIND BROCCOLI STEM SOUP

This just-spicy-enough soup is magical for a few reasons. First, despite being velvety smooth and luxuriously creamy, it's completely vegan. Second, while it takes a little time to cook (the tough broccoli stems and cashews need to simmer in the bubbling broth in order to develop flavor and fully break down so they purée nicely), it could not be easier to make. You just chop, sauté, add liquid, cook, then blend. Third, and perhaps most magical, this recipe embodies "kind" in the most Grateful Dead sense of the word: It gives new life to vegetable scraps (broccoli and cilantro stems), saving them from being wasted, turning them into so much more than the sum of their parts—kind to Mother Earth, your belly, and taste buds in equal measure.

YIELD: 4 SERVINGS

2 tablespoons neutral oil, such as canola, vegetable, or avocado

1 medium white or yellow onion, chopped

1-inch piece fresh ginger, chopped

3 cloves garlic, smashed

1½ teaspoons yellow curry powder

About 5 long stems broccoli, florets removed, chopped into 1-inch pieces

⅛ cup raw cashews

3 cups vegetable broth

1 tablespoon sriracha, more or less to taste

½ to ¾ teaspoon salt, depending on the salinity of the liquid used

Stems from 1 bunch fresh cilantro, plus a handful of leaves for garnish

Heat the oil over medium heat in a heavy-bottomed pot. Add the onion and cook for 3 to 4 minutes, until softened and translucent. Add the ginger, garlic, curry powder, and broccoli stems and cook for 2 to 3 minutes, stirring occasionally, until very fragrant. Turn down the heat if it starts to smoke or scorch. Add the cashews and broth.

Reduce the heat to medium-low and simmer for 45 minutes to 1 hour, until the broccoli stems are very soft.

Purée with an immersion blender or in a food processor or blender until very smooth. Run for at least a couple of minutes, until the cashews get creamy and emulsify the soup and the broccoli stems fully break down. Add the sriracha and salt as needed, as well as the cilantro stems. Purée again just until the cilantro stems break down. The soup should have tiny green flecks.

Serve hot, garnished with cilantro leaves and/or more sriracha if desired.

VEGGIE TORTILLA SOUP

Traditional tortilla soup, a.k.a. sopa Azteca, may normally contain shredded chicken, but even without it, this one hits all the same notes and satisfies cravings for the iconic Mexican dish: smoky, spicy, tomatoey and lots of mix-ins (in this case, red bell peppers, diced carrots, and pinto and/or black beans, plus lots of crispy tortilla strips). Because it's so hearty, this is a good one to serve as the centerpiece of a meal, perhaps with a simple green salad or slaw on the side and something cold and refreshing to drink.

YIELD: 4 SERVINGS

3 tablespoons neutral oil, such as avocado or grapeseed oil

1 large or 2 medium yellow onions, chopped

1½ teaspoons chili powder

2 teaspoons ground cumin

1 teaspoon kosher salt, or more to taste

4 cloves garlic, finely minced

1 or 2 canned chipotle peppers in adobo, finely chopped, plus 1 or 2 spoonfuls of their sauce, or more to taste

One 15-ounce can crushed tomatoes

4 cups vegetable broth or prepared vegetable bouillon

1 medium red bell pepper, seeded and chopped

2 medium carrots, peeled and finely diced

Two 15-ounce cans pinto or black beans (or one of each), drained and rinsed

Four 6-inch corn tortillas, cut into long ½-inch-wide strips

1 large handful fresh cilantro, chopped (about ¼ cup chopped), plus more for garnish

Zest and juice of 1 lime

FOR GARNISH (OPTIONAL)

Sour cream or Greek yogurt (dairy of plant based)

Sliced avocado

Thinly sliced radishes

Quick-Pickled Onions (page 41)

Heat a large (4- to 6-quart) pot with a fitted lid over medium heat and add 2 tablespoons of the oil. Then add the onions and sauté until translucent and fragrant, 3 to 4 minutes. Add the chili powder, cumin, ½ teaspoon of the salt, garlic, chipotle peppers and sauce, and crushed tomatoes. Reduce the heat to medium-low and cook for 5 to 6 minutes, stirring occasionally. The tomato mixture should reduce to a thick, concentrated paste.

Add the broth. Then stir in the bell pepper, carrots, and the remaining ½ teaspoon salt. Cover the pot, bring the heat up to medium-high, and bring the soup to a boil. Once boiling, reduce the heat to medium-low and let simmer for 25 to 30 minutes, until the vegetables are very tender. Stir in the beans, taste the broth, and add more salt if necessary.

While the soup cooks, preheat the oven to 400°F.

Put the tortilla strips in a small mixing bowl and pour the remaining 1 tablespoon oil over them. Use your hands to gently toss, making sure they are well coated, and sprinkle with the remaining ¼ teaspoon salt. Transfer the tortilla strips to a rimmed baking sheet and bake for 9 to 11 minutes, tossing halfway through, until the tortilla strips are crisp and golden brown.

Stir the cilantro into the soup, saving some for garnish, and add the lime zest and juice.

Ladle the soup into bowls and top with the crispy tortilla strips, more cilantro, and any garnishes you choose. Store leftovers in an airtight container in the refrigerator for up to 4 days.

SPICY CORN CHOWDER

It's been said that, while not everyone likes the Grateful Dead, the people who do like them *really* like them. Whether that theory also applies to capsaicin (the chemical compound in chiles that causes their burning sensation) is up for debate. Fortunately, this spicy take on classic corn chowder can easily be adjusted to suit your heat tolerance levels. Prefer a milder soup? Use less jalapeño and chipotle peppers (or omit them altogether). On the other hand, if your feelings about the hurts-so-good tingle of spicy food more closely mirrors the way Dead Heads feel about the Dead, then by all means, bump it up as much as you can handle and add a few dashes of hot sauce for good measure!

YIELD: 4 SERVINGS

1 tablespoon extra-virgin olive oil

1 medium yellow onion, chopped

½ teaspoon kosher salt, or more to taste

3 cloves garlic, finely chopped

3 ribs celery, sliced

1 medium Yukon gold or russet potato, scrubbed and diced (about 1 cup diced)

Kernels from 4 medium ears fresh corn or 3 cups frozen corn

1 red bell pepper, seeded and diced

1 jalapeño, seeded and diced (leave the seeds intact for spicier soup)

1 or 2 canned chipotle peppers packed in adobo, or more to taste, chopped

½ teaspoon smoked paprika

1 tablespoon white wine vinegar

2½ cups vegetable broth or prepared bouillon

1½ cups half-and-half (or one 14-ounce can coconut milk)

Freshly ground black pepper

1 handful fresh cilantro or thinly sliced green onion, for garnish

Heat the olive oil in a large, heavy-bottomed pot over medium heat. Add the onion and salt. Cook until softened and translucent, 4 to 5 minutes.

Stir in the garlic, celery, potato, corn kernels, red pepper, jalapeño, chipotle pepper, and smoked paprika. Cook until the potato is slightly softened, about 5 minutes. Add the vinegar, broth, and half-and-half. Taste and add more salt and pepper as needed.

Cover, reduce the heat to medium-low, and simmer for 15 more minutes, until the potato is tender. Remove about one-third of the soup and let cool for 10 minutes, then transfer to a blender or food processor. Process until smooth, then return it to the pot and stir (you may also do this by pulsing an immersion blender in the pot a few times).

Taste and adjust the seasonings as needed, then ladle into bowls and serve, garnished with the cilantro.

CHICKEN(LESS) PHO

It's hard to beat a big, steaming bowl of pho, resplendent with chewy rice vermicelli noodles and lots of fresh garnishes. Every bite simultaneously soothes your soul and awakens your senses. This vegetarian take on chicken pho gets its rich, umami flavor from a broth made with vegetables and spices.

YIELD: 4 SERVINGS

FOR THE BROTH

1 tablespoon neutral oil, such as avocado or grapeseed oil

2-inch piece fresh ginger, roughly chopped

2 whole star anise pods or ½ teaspoon ground star anise

1 cinnamon stick or 1 teaspoon ground cinnamon

2 whole cloves or ⅛ teaspoon ground cloves

2 medium yellow onions, cut into quarters

3 tablespoons nutritional yeast

6 cloves garlic, smashed

3 medium carrots, scrubbed and chopped into 2-inch pieces

8 cups water

1 to 2 teaspoons honey or maple syrup

2½ teaspoons kosher salt, or more to taste

1 tablespoon rice vinegar

FOR THE TOFU

2 tablespoons neutral oil, such as avocado or grapeseed oil, plus more as needed

One 12-ounce package extra-firm tofu, drained, patted dry, and cut into ½-inch cubes

Kosher salt

FOR THE NOODLES

8 ounces dried rice vermicelli

FOR GARNISH

1 green jalapeño, thinly sliced

Thai basil and/or fresh cilantro leaves

White onion, thinly sliced

Sriracha and hoisin sauce (optional)

To make the broth: Heat the oil in a large pot over medium heat. Add the ginger, star anise, cinnamon stick, and cloves. Stir well. Then add the onion and nutritional yeast and cook, stirring occasionally, for 4 to 5 minutes, until the onion begins to turn brown. Add the garlic and cook for another 1 to 2 minutes, until softened. Add the carrots, water, honey, and salt. Stir well. Raise the heat to high and cover the pot to bring to a boil.

Once boiling, reduce the heat to low and simmer, covered, for 1 hour.

To make the tofu: In the final 30 minutes of broth cooking time, heat the oil in a large, heavy-bottomed frying pan over medium-high heat. Add the cubed tofu and fry for 3 to 4 minutes on each side, adding more oil if necessary, until lightly crisp. Drain the tofu on paper towels and salt lightly. Set aside.

To make the noodles: Bring a medium pot of water to a boil and cook the rice vermicelli according to the package instructions. Drain and rinse with cool water to stop the cooking. Cover the noodles until ready to use.

Strain the broth using a colander and return it to the pot. Add the vinegar. Taste for salt and add more if necessary. If the broth reduced too much during cooking and is too salty, add a bit more water. Cover the broth to keep it hot.

Divide the noodles among four bowls and ladle the broth into each one. Divide the fried tofu among the bowls. Then garnish each bowl with your choice of toppings. Serve with sriracha and hoisin sauce at the table, if desired.

EGGPLANT-SPINACH DUMPLING SOUP

Each bowl of this flavorful soup is brimming with tender little eggplant-spinach dumplings, which, despite being completely vegan, are satisfying even to carnivores, thanks to eggplant's meaty texture and proclivity for absorbing whatever flavors you add to it. (Or, if you're in the mood for dumpling soup but are short on time or patience, use your favorite frozen dumplings instead.)

YIELD: 4 SERVINGS

FOR THE DUMPLINGS

- 1 tablespoon neutral oil, such as avocado or grapeseed oil
- 2 shallots or 1 medium yellow onion, finely diced
- 1 medium eggplant, finely diced
- 3 cloves garlic, minced
- 1-inch piece fresh ginger, minced
- 2 cups fresh baby spinach, roughly chopped
- 2 tablespoons soy sauce, tamari, or coconut aminos
- 1 to 2 teaspoons sriracha or other chili-garlic hot sauce
- 1 teaspoon toasted sesame oil
- All-purpose flour, for dusting
- 24 small square wonton wrappers

FOR THE BROTH

- 6 cups vegetable broth or prepared vegetable bouillon
- 1 to 2 tablespoons soy sauce, tamari, or coconut aminos
- ½ teaspoon kosher salt, more or less to taste
- 2 teaspoons toasted sesame oil
- 1-inch piece fresh ginger, chopped
- 4 cloves garlic, smashed with a knife

FOR SERVING

- 3 green onions, sliced
- Red pepper flakes or Spicy-Crunchy Chili Oil (page 40)

To make the dumplings: In a large frying pan, heat the oil over medium heat. Add the shallots and cook, stirring frequently, for 3 to 4 minutes, until translucent and fragrant. Add the eggplant, garlic, and ginger and cook, stirring occasionally, for 5 to 6 minutes, until the eggplant is softened.

Add the spinach, soy sauce, and sriracha and cook, stirring occasionally, for another 2 to 3 minutes, until the spinach has completely wilted and the soy sauce has been absorbed into the vegetables. Transfer the mixture to a large plate or rimmed baking sheet to cool completely.

To make the broth: While the mixture cools, combine the broth ingredients in a 4- to 6-quart pot. Stir well, cover, and turn the heat to high. Bring the soup to a boil, then reduce the heat to medium-low and simmer for 20 to 25 minutes. Strain out any solids and discard. Keep the broth covered with the heat off until ready to add the dumplings.

To assemble the dumplings: Lightly flour a clean, dry surface and set the stack of wonton wrappers on it, covered with a clean kitchen towel to keep them from drying out. Fill a small bowl with water and set it on your workspace. Lightly flour (or line with parchment paper or a silicone mat) a rimmed baking sheet or large plate.

Take a wrapper out of the stack and set it in front of you, then use a pastry brush or your fingers to coat the edges lightly with water.

Spoon about 1½ tablespoons of the filling in the center of each wrapper. Gently pinch the corners together to form a point and tightly seal the edges to lock in the filling. Make sure to press the air out of the middle of the dumpling to form a tight, neat package. Transfer the dumpling to the prepared baking sheet. Repeat to make 24 dumplings.

Bring the broth to a simmer over medium-low heat. Taste the broth and adjust the seasonings as necessary. Add the dumplings and cook until they float and the wrappers appear nearly translucent, 5 to 6 minutes.

To serve: Ladle the soup into bowls and garnish with the sliced green onions and a small pinch of red pepper flakes.

WATERMELON GAZPACHO

If you're looking for a unique show-stopper to start a meal, look no further than this chilled watermelon gazpacho, which is practically as easy as making a smoothie (put a bunch of produce in a blender, blitz it up, and pour).

YIELD: 4 SERVINGS

2 baby seedless watermelons

2 cups tomato juice

2 medium cloves garlic

1 large handful fresh cilantro leaves, plus more for garnish

1 small handful fresh mint leaves, plus more for garnish

½ red onion, finely diced

1 English cucumber, peeled, seeded, and finely chopped (or use 2 or 3 small Persian cucumbers)

1 medium red bell pepper, seeded and finely chopped

Juice of 2 limes

2 tablespoons extra-virgin olive oil, plus more for garnish

1 tablespoon plus 2 teaspoons balsamic vinegar

¼ teaspoon kosher salt, or more to taste

A few grinds black pepper, plus more for garnish

Cut each watermelon in half to make two "bowls" and slice a very thin piece of the rind off each one to make a flat bottom so the watermelon can serve as a bowl without tipping over.

Use a large spoon to scrape all but about ⅛ inch of the watermelon flesh out of the rind and transfer it to a bowl. Take care not to make any holes in the bottom of the watermelon "bowl." If you notice any black seeds, remove them.

Place the scooped-out watermelon flesh, tomato juice, garlic, cilantro, mint, and half of each of the onion, cucumber, and bell pepper in a blender or food processor. Add the lime juice, olive oil, vinegar, salt, and pepper and pulse a few times. The gazpacho should be mostly smooth with a few chunks. Depending on the size of your blender or food processor, you may need to work in batches.

Combine the remaining onion, cucumber, and bell pepper in a medium bowl and mix well.

Chill the watermelon "bowls," puréed soup, and chopped vegetables until ready to serve.

Divide the soup among the watermelon "bowls." Then add one-fourth of the chopped vegetables to each one. Serve immediately, garnished with a drizzle of olive oil and more pepper.

RED LENTIL SOUP WITH LIME AND CILANTRO

This hearty lentil soup has a lot in common with traditional lentil soup, popularized in the 1970s: lentils, a pleasantly heady cumin aroma, onions, tomatoes, and carrots—all longtime pals of the lentil. Here, red lentils are used in place of the usual green, and ginger, lime, and fresh cilantro brighten the whole thing up.

YIELD: 4–6 SERVINGS

3 tablespoons extra-virgin olive oil

1 large yellow onion, chopped

2 cloves garlic, chopped

½-inch piece fresh ginger, grated

1 teaspoon ground cumin

½ teaspoon smoked paprika

½ teaspoon ground coriander

½ teaspoon kosher salt, or more to taste

A few grinds black pepper

One 15-ounce can crushed tomatoes

6 cups vegetable broth (or vegetable bouillon dissolved in water)

1 cup red lentils

3 medium carrots, peeled and diced

Juice of 1 lime, plus more for garnish

1 large handful fresh cilantro, chopped (about ½ cup chopped), plus more for garnish

Plain Greek yogurt (dairy or plant based) or Cashew Crema (page 46), for serving

Heat a large 4- or 6-quart pot over high heat and add the olive oil. Add the onion, garlic, and ginger and sauté until they soften and begin to brown, about 3 minutes.

Stir in the cumin, smoked paprika, coriander, salt, and pepper and cook for 2 minutes longer.

Add the crushed tomatoes, broth, lentils, and carrots. Cover the pot and cook over low heat until the lentils and carrots are soft, 25 to 30 minutes. Taste, then adjust the salt and pepper as needed.

Just before serving, stir in the lime juice and cilantro. Ladle the soup into bowls and garnish with a dollop of yogurt and more lime juice and/or cilantro.

SESAME SLAW WITH PEANUTS

This enormous salad is an ideal side for just about any meal, but it's also a whole lot of potential in a (very big) bowl as a main course. It'll accommodate any protein (crispy tofu, grilled tempeh, even barbecued or roasted mushrooms), tastes delicious tucked into a large tortilla or pita, and can be tossed with oven-crisped leftover rice or tender rice noodles. It's endlessly customizable. Switch the veggies, the nuts and seeds, or even the dressing. All are excellent with the Coconut-Curry Dressing on page 44. And should you decide you don't feel like dusting off your knives and prefer to make this with bagged slaw mix instead? It'll still be delicious.

YIELD: 4–6 SERVINGS

4 carrots, peeled and shredded or thinly sliced

1 English or 4 Persian cucumbers, thinly sliced into half-moons

4 ribs celery, thinly sliced

1 red bell pepper, seeded and thinly sliced

2 cup thinly sliced cabbage (any kind—napa, red, green, savoy)

6 green onions, thinly sliced

1 cup green grapes, halved

1 cup Miso-Sesame Dressing (page 51)

¾ cup roasted, salted peanuts, chopped

1 large handful fresh cilantro stems and leaves, chopped (about ½ cup chopped)

3 tablespoons toasted sesame seeds

Combine the vegetables and grapes in a large serving bowl. Pour the dressing over the top and toss well to combine. Scatter most of the peanuts and cilantro (reserve a couple tablespoons of each for garnish) and 2 tablespoons of the toasted sesame seeds over the top and toss gently a few times to combine. Top with the remaining peanuts, cilantro, and sesame seeds. Serve immediately.

GREEN GODDESS CAESAR WITH CRISPY TOFU CROUTONS

As you scan the ingredients listed in this recipe, you might be thinking to yourself, *Um. I've had Caesar salad before, and this does not sound like Caesar salad.* Well, you're not wrong, but rest assured, this salad will not only satisfy any classic Caesar salad cravings you might have, but it'll also have you rethinking the salad as a concept. Though Caesar dressing—usually made with lemon juice, Dijon mustard, an egg, anchovies, and garlic—and green goddess dressing are different, they do share the flavor profile of creamy-salty-funky, and for that reason, this salad more than works. And while typical Caesars are topped with crunchy, garlicky croutons, this salad is topped with crunchy, garlicky *tofu* croutons, which, in addition to adding crispy texture and great flavor to the salad, give it a big boost of protein, making it a great full-meal salad when served in a larger portion.

YIELD: 4–6 SERVINGS

FOR THE TOFU CROUTONS

One 16-ounce package extra-firm tofu, drained, patted dry, and cut into 1-inch cubes

3 tablespoons extra-virgin olive oil, plus more for the pan

2 tablespoons nutritional yeast

2 tablespoons cornstarch

½ teaspoon garlic powder

¼ teaspoon kosher salt

Several grinds black pepper

FOR THE SALAD

3 large romaine hearts, sliced or torn into large bite-size pieces

½ cup Vegan Green Goddess Dressing (page 47)

¼ cup freshly grated Parmesan cheese (dairy or plant based) or ¼ cup Walnut-Cashew Parmesan (page 52)

Preheat the oven to 425°F. Line a rimmed baking sheet with parchment paper or a silicone baking mat or grease lightly with olive oil.

To make the tofu croutons: Place the tofu in a large mixing bowl and pour the olive oil over it. Mix well using your hands or a rubber spatula to ensure each cube is well coated. Combine the nutritional yeast, cornstarch, garlic powder, salt, and pepper in a small bowl and mix well. Pour the dry mixture over the oiled tofu cubes and toss well to coat,

Spread the tofu on the prepared baking sheet. Bake for 10 to 12 minutes, until the tofu bottoms turn golden brown and crispy. Remove the pan from the oven and carefully flip each tofu cube over. Return to the oven and bake for another 10 to 12 minutes, until the cubes are nicely browned and crisp on both sides.

To make the salad: Arrange the lettuce in a large bowl and pour the green goddess dressing over the top. Toss well to coat. Sprinkle on almost all of the cheese (reserve a couple teaspoons for garnish).

If serving in a large bowl, add the tofu to the bowl and sprinkle on the rest of the cheese. If plating the salads individually, top each with the tofu and remaining cheese. Serve immediately.

MANGO-AVOCADO SALAD

This juicy salad hardly needs any dressing, but the tangy lime-and-olive-oil one it's tossed with puts it over the top. Don't skip the nuts on top, but feel free to use any others. Roasted cashews or toasted, slivered almonds are also nice.

YIELD: 4 SERVINGS

2 tablespoons neutral oil, such as avocado or grapeseed oil

One 16-ounce package extra-firm tofu, drained, patted dry, and cut into ½-inch cubes

¾ teaspoon kosher salt

Zest and juice of 2 medium limes

2 tablespoons extra-virgin olive oil

2 teaspoons maple syrup or honey

1 ripe avocado, peeled, halved, pitted, and diced

1 ripe mango, peeled, pitted, and diced

2 carrots, peeled and shredded

4 green onions, sliced

½ medium red onion, diced

2 cups cherry or grape tomatoes, halved

1 large handful fresh mint, torn (about ¼ cup torn)

¼ cup roasted, salted peanuts, chopped

Heat the neutral oil in a medium frying pan over medium-high heat. Add the tofu and fry for 3 to 5 minutes, until crisp and brown; flip and brown at least one other side. Transfer the tofu to paper towels to drain and sprinkle with ½ teaspoon of the salt. Let it cool while you prepare the rest of the salad.

In a small bowl, whisk together the lime zest and juice, olive oil, maple syrup, and remaining ¼ teaspoon salt. Set aside.

In a serving bowl, toss together the avocado, mango, carrots, green onions, red onion, tomatoes, and mint. Pour the dressing over the top and toss well. Top the salad with the tofu and peanuts and serve.

LEMONY FARRO AND CHARD SALAD

This nourishing salad may be served warm or at room temperature and is just the thing when the weather turns blustery. Featuring two whole bunches of chard, plus chewy toasted farro, a zippy lemon dressing, and juicy pomegranate seeds, it's a big chorus of flavor in one bowl.

YIELD: 4 SERVINGS

3 cups water

1½ cups farro, rinsed

1 teaspoon kosher salt

2 tablespoons extra-virgin olive oil

1 medium red onion, diced

4 cloves garlic, thinly sliced

1½ pounds chard (e.g., Swiss chard, rainbow chard, red chard), leaves roughly chopped and stems thinly sliced

¼ cup Whole Lemon Vinaigrette (page 50)

A few grinds black pepper

¼ cup freshly grated Parmesan (dairy or plant based) or Cashew-Walnut Parmesan (page 52)

½ cup pomegranate seeds (from 1 medium pomegranate)

In a medium pot, combine the water, farro, and salt. Cover and bring to a boil, then reduce to a simmer. Cook, covered, for 25 minutes, until the water is absorbed and the farro is tender.

Heat the olive oil in a large, heavy-bottomed frying pan over medium heat and add the onion. Sauté for 3 to 4 minutes, until translucent and fragrant, then add the garlic. Cook, stirring occasionally, until the garlic is tender and fragrant, 1 minute.

Add the chopped chard stems to the pan and cook until softened, about 4 minutes. Add the farro to the pan and continue to toss until the farro, aromatics, and chard stems are well combined. Cook for 1 to 2 minutes to allow the farro to toast, then remove the pan from the heat.

Put the chard leaves in the bottom of a serving bowl and pour the hot farro and chard stem mixture over the top. Let sit for 5 minutes, then pour the lemon dressing over the top and toss well to combine the farro, stems, leaves, and dressing.

Top with the pepper, Parmesan, and pomegranate seeds and serve warm or at room temperature.

ROASTED BROCCOLI RABE AND CARROT SALAD

Though it looks somewhat like baby broccoli or a flowering broccoli plant, broccoli rabe, sometimes called rapini, is actually more closely related to the turnip. It may seem intimidating at first, but its earthy, bitter flavor is quite delicious once you tame it a bit and balance it with bright flavors and proper seasoning. Here, the rabe is blanched and then roasted along with sliced carrots, lots of garlic, and olive oil. The roasting both tenderizes the tougher stalks and helps dial back just enough of the bitterness so it doesn't overpower the whole dish. A large handful of creamy feta (dairy or plant based) or goat cheese helps pull the whole thing together, but you can go in a different direction and top it with toasted walnuts or almonds or even a bit of chopped preserved lemon.

YIELD: 4 SERVINGS

One 12-ounce bunch broccoli rabe, ends trimmed

8 carrots, peeled and thinly sliced

1 medium white or yellow onion, sliced

4 cloves garlic, finely minced

2 tablespoons extra-virgin olive oil

Zest and juice of 1 lemon

½ teaspoon kosher salt, plus more for salting the water

½ teaspoon freshly ground black pepper

4 ounces crumbled goat cheese or feta (dairy or plant based)

Preheat the oven to 400°F.

Bring a pot of salted water to a boil. Add the broccoli rabe and cook until the stems are tender, about 2 minutes. Drain.

Spread the carrot slices, onion, cooked rabe, and garlic on a baking sheet. Drizzle with the olive oil and use your fingers to coat the vegetables well with the oil.

Roast for 20 to 25 minutes, or until the carrots are cooked and the onion browns slightly. Transfer to a serving platter and refrigerate for 15 to 20 minutes to bring the temperature down.

To serve, toss with the lemon zest and juice, salt, and pepper. Top with the crumbled cheese.

SIDE PLAYERS

ACCOMPANIMENTS

The Grateful Dead knew sides mattered and deserved not only special attention but also reverence. They knew that sometimes the sides were one of the most important parts of the show.

Similarly, when you're focused on executing a whole meal, it can be tempting to spend the bulk of your time and energy on the main course. If you run out of time, you figure you'll just throw a store-bought loaf of bread and a bagged salad on the table at the last minute and call it a day. But the band's understanding of the importance of sides is wise to emulate here. When you add a side dish to a meal, it should not only complement the main course but also add its own value, setting the whole meal apart. When you eat the side dish with the other food on your plate, the whole thing should harmonize.

Serve the sides in this chapter with the entrées in later chapters or make like a vegetarian at a carnivore's Thanksgiving table, and make a whole meal of sides.

BROWN BUTTER-GOCHUJANG BRUSSELS SPROUTS

This recipe contains multiple layers of flavor—nutty brown butter, spicy-sweet gochujang (a fermented Korean hot pepper paste), tangy lemon, juicy pomegranate seeds, and crunchy toasted almonds—and they all come together to create something entirely new. Each component is essential for the complete dish to work, but they need each other to really sing.

YIELD: 4–6 SERVINGS

2 pounds brussels sprouts, ends trimmed and halved

2 tablespoons extra-virgin olive oil

½ teaspoon kosher salt

¼ cup unsalted butter (dairy or plant based)

3 tablespoons gochujang (substitute sriracha if you cannot find it)

2 tablespoons honey or maple syrup

Zest and juice of ½ lemon

3 green onions, sliced thinly

¼ cup sliced, toasted almonds

Seeds from 1 small or ½ large pomegranate (about ½ cup seeds)

Preheat the oven to 475°F.

In a large mixing bowl, combine the brussels sprouts with the oil and salt. Divide the sprouts between two ungreased rimmed baking sheets and roast until tender and browned, 16 to 18 minutes.

Melt the butter in a small saucepan over medium heat. When it has melted, reduce the heat to medium-low and allow the butter to brown. Watch it carefully and remove from the heat when the butter begins to smell nutty, about 5 minutes. Whisk in the gochujang, honey, and lemon zest and juice to create a thick, syrupy sauce.

Pour the sauce over the roasted brussels sprouts and mix gently to coat.

Transfer to a platter and top with the green onions, sliced almonds, and pomegranate seeds. Toss gently and serve.

CRISPY SWEET POTATO OVEN FRIES

This is the sort of side dish you'll immediately wish you made twice as much of because it's just that crave-ably good. While it can certainly be prepared using regular potatoes (russets work best) or red garnet yams, the mash-up between oven-caramelized, just-sweet-enough Muraski sweet potatoes (the kind with super-firm white flesh and rust-colored skins), lots of fresh garlic and parsley, plus olive oil and salty Parmesan is hard to beat. Serve these with burgers and sandwiches, tuck them into a shawarma wrap, or even serve as a stand-in for breakfast potatoes alongside a tofu scramble or omelet.

YIELD: 4–6 SERVINGS

- 4 medium sweet potatoes (preferably the red-skinned Muraski variety), cut into thin fries
- 6 tablespoons extra-virgin olive oil
- 1 teaspoon kosher salt
- 4 cloves garlic, finely minced
- ¼ cup grated Parmesan (dairy or plant based) or Walnut-Cashew Parmesan (page 52)
- 1 large handful fresh parsley, chopped (about ½ cup chopped)
- 1 teaspoon red pepper flakes, or more to taste

Preheat the oven to 400°F. Arrange two oven racks as close to the center of the oven as possible.

In a large bowl, combine the sweet potatoes with 4 tablespoons of the olive oil and the salt. Divide between two rimmed baking sheets and spread out the sweet potatoes so they are not touching each other.

Bake for 20 minutes on one side. Remove the trays from the oven and flip the sweet potatoes. Return the trays to the oven, switching locations to encourage even cooking.

Bake for another 12 to 14 minutes, until brown and crispy.

Cool the sweet potatoes for 5 minutes. This step is crucial, as it helps further crisp the potatoes.

While the sweet potatoes cool, combine the remaining 2 tablespoons olive oil, garlic, Parmesan, parsley, and red pepper flakes in a small bowl. Drizzle the oil mixture over the top of the fries and toss well to coat.

Transfer to a serving platter and serve immediately.

COCONUT RICE

Warning: Once you discover how easy it is to make coconut rice (nearly as easy as making plain rice), you may start questioning why you don't put a can of coconut milk in *every* batch of rice you cook. The salt and sweetener (your choice of maple syrup or honey) in this just-rich-enough coconut rice don't overpower it; they serve to bring out the coconut milk's flavor, and although the crispy shallots and lime zest and juice aren't required, they bring beautiful balance to the rice.

Serve this in place of the rice in the Black Pepper Tofu and Asparagus Rice Bowls on page 133, beneath a generous serving of the Spicy Chickpea Curry on page 135, or with any stir-fry, curry, grilled vegetables, or tofu.

YIELD: 4 SERVINGS

1½ cups jasmine rice, rinsed

One 14-ounce can full-fat coconut milk

½ cup water

½ teaspoon kosher salt, or more to taste

1 teaspoon maple syrup or honey

3 tablespoons neutral oil, such as avocado or grapeseed oil

2 medium shallots, thinly sliced (optional)

Zest and juice of 1 lime (optional)

Combine the rice, coconut milk, water, salt, and maple syrup in a pot and bring to a boil over high heat. Cover, reduce the heat to low, and simmer for 15 minutes, or until the liquid is absorbed.

While the rice cooks, heat the oil in a medium frying pan over medium heat and fry the shallots for 5 to 6 minutes, until golden and crisp (don't be tempted to turn up the heat—they'll brown too quickly). Drain on paper towels or a cooling rack (this will crisp them further) and sprinkle lightly with salt.

When the rice finishes cooking, shut off the heat and let it sit, covered, for 10 minutes. Fluff the rice with a fork and stir in the lime zest and juice, if using. Top with the crispy shallots, if using, and serve hot.

NOTE: If you want to cook the rice in a rice cooker or an electric pressure cooker like an Instant Pot, place the rice, ¼ cup water, coconut milk, salt, and maple syrup in the rice cooker or electric pressure cooker and stir well. If using a rice cooker, set to Cook. If using an electric pressure cooker, set to Rice or pressure-cook on high for 12 minutes. Then proceed with the shallots.

TOMATO RICE

Think of this red-hued, spiced rice dish as a simplified version of what you may know as Mexican or Spanish rice. Use it in Kind Veggie Bean and Cheese Burritos (page 18); as a landing pad for beans, cheese, guacamole, and vegetables in Kind Burrito Bowls (page 130); or as an ideal side dish for tacos or enchiladas. It can also accommodate any veggies you like: ½ cup fresh or frozen corn kernels, diced red bell pepper or fresh jalapeños, finely diced carrot, or green peas. They all fit in beautifully.

YIELD: 4 SERVINGS

2 tablespoons unsalted butter (dairy or plant based) or neutral oil, such as avocado or grapeseed oil

1 medium yellow onion, finely diced

2 cloves garlic, minced

1½ cups long-grain white rice, such as basmati, Texmati, or jasmine

½ teaspoon chili powder

¼ teaspoon ground cumin

One 15-ounce can crushed tomatoes

1 tablespoon tomato paste

2 cups vegetable broth, prepared vegetable bouillon, or tomato bouillon

½ teaspoon salt, or more to taste

1 small handful fresh cilantro leaves or 2 green onions, thinly sliced

Heat a medium pot over medium heat and add the butter to melt. Add the onion and cook for 2 to 3 minutes, until translucent, then stir in the garlic and cook for another minute, just until fragrant.

Add the rice, chili powder, and cumin to the onion-garlic mixture. Stir frequently with a wooden spoon. The rice should begin to toast slightly and the mixture will become quite fragrant.

Add the crushed tomatoes, tomato paste, broth, and salt to the pot and stir well to combine. Use the wooden spoon to scrape any stuck-on bits from the bottom of the pan and incorporate them into the rice-liquid mixture. Cover the pot, raise the heat to high, and bring to a boil. Once boiling, reduce the heat to low.

Let the rice simmer, covered, for 20 minutes. Then shut off the heat and let the rice sit, still covered, for 5 minutes. Fluff the rice with a fork and garnish with the cilantro leaves.

NOTE: If you want to cook the rice in a rice cooker or an electric pressure cooker like an Instant Pot, combine all the ingredients except the cilantro or green onions in the rice cooker or electric pressure cooker and stir well. If using a rice cooker, set to Cook; if using an electric pressure cooker, set to Rice or pressure-cook on high for 12 minutes.

SESAME NOODLES WITH PICKLED CARROTS AND CUCUMBERS

This highly slurpable dish of chewy noodles tossed in a creamy sesame-peanut sauce and topped with fridge-pickled vegetables, toasted sesame seeds, a shower of roasted peanuts, and green onions is an ideal addition to the table when you're celebrating something great, but it's also an excellent panacea for a truly terrible day. After a bowlful (or three), you're certain to find yourself in a much-improved mood. If you want to serve these noodles as a main course, add cubed, pan-fried tofu or seitan-based vegan chicken on top.

YIELD: 4 SERVINGS

6 tablespoons rice vinegar

2 tablespoons maple syrup or honey

1 teaspoon kosher salt

½ cup cold water

½ English cucumber or 1 Persian cucumber, cut into thin matchsticks (no need to peel)

2 medium carrots, peeled and cut into matchsticks

2 tablespoons toasted sesame oil

3 tablespoons soy sauce or tamari (you may also use coconut aminos, but you'll likely need to add a bit of salt and reduce the sweetener)

2 tablespoons Chinese sesame paste or tahini

2 tablespoons smooth peanut butter

1-inch piece fresh ginger, grated or finely minced

2 cloves garlic, grated or finely minced

1 to 3 teaspoons chili-garlic sauce, sriracha, store-bought chili oil, or Spicy-Crunchy Chili Oil (page 40), plus more for garnish

16 ounces Chinese wheat noodles, udon, or linguine

2 tablespoons toasted sesame seeds

¼ cup salted, roasted peanuts, chopped

3 green onions, thinly sliced

Combine 4 tablespoons of the rice vinegar, 1 tablespoon of the maple syrup, the salt, and water in a medium bowl or other container, preferably one with a fitted lid. Add the cucumber and carrots, cover, and refrigerate while you cook the noodles and prepare the sauce. This step may be done up to 3 days in advance.

In a medium bowl, whisk together the sesame oil, soy sauce, remaining 2 tablespoons rice vinegar, sesame paste, peanut butter, remaining 1 tablespoon maple syrup, ginger, garlic, and chili-garlic sauce. Taste and adjust the seasoning as needed.

Bring a large pot of water to a boil over high heat. Add the noodles and cook according to the package instructions. Drain the noodles, rinse with cold water to stop the cooking, and transfer to a large mixing bowl.

Pour the sauce over the noodles and toss well to combine. Add the toasted sesame seeds and toss again to distribute. Transfer to a serving bowl or platter.

Drain the cucumber and carrots and scatter them across the top of the sauced noodles. Garnish with the chopped peanuts, green onions, and more chili-garlic sauce and serve.

SRIRACHA-MAPLE ROASTED CARROTS

These lightly sweet, slightly spicy, very, *very* good roasted carrots may be a bit more sophisticated, more complex, and a whole lot prettier than carrots cooked with butter and brown sugar—the classic side dish on which they are based—but they are just as easy to make. They can also be prepared with any hot sauce and sweetener you like. Other good combinations are a chipotle-based hot sauce with agave or a cayenne and vinegar hot sauce, such as Frank's RedHot or Tabasco, with honey.

YIELD: 4–6 SERVINGS

3 pounds carrots, cut into 3- to 4-inch lengths, or baby carrots sold with the tender green stems intact

2 tablespoons extra-virgin olive oil

½ teaspoon kosher salt, or more to taste

A few grinds black pepper

3 tablespoons unsalted butter (dairy or plant based), melted

1 tablespoon sriracha, or more to taste

1 tablespoon maple syrup, or more to taste

2 green onions, thinly sliced, or a handful fresh cilantro, finely chopped, for garnish (optional)

Preheat the oven to 375°F.

Combine the carrots and olive oil in a large bowl. Use your hands or a wooden spoon to toss well, ensuring the carrots are well coated. Season with the salt and pepper and toss again.

Spread the carrots out evenly on a rimmed baking sheet. Roast for 18 minutes, rotating the pan halfway through.

While the carrots roast, stir together the melted butter, sriracha, and maple syrup in a small bowl.

After 18 minutes, remove the carrots from the oven. Pour the butter-sriracha-maple mixture over them and toss well. Return to the oven for 3 to 5 minutes to allow the sauce to thicken slightly.

Transfer to a platter, top with the green onions, if using, and serve warm.

COCONUT-KALE RED LENTIL DAL

While this nutritious, ultraflavorful dal is technically a side dish, it could easily become the main event at a meal, perhaps served over rice and with some warm flatbread. If you really want to gild the lily (and who doesn't?), add a dollop of yogurt (full-fat Greek or coconut-based yogurts are quite good here, or use Cashew Crema, page 46).

YIELD: 4 SERVINGS

- 3 tablespoons coconut oil, neutral oil, such as avocado or grapeseed oil, or ghee (clarified butter)
- 1 teaspoon cumin seeds or ¼ teaspoon ground cumin
- 1 teaspoon fennel seed
- 1 teaspoon ground turmeric
- 2 medium red onions, diced
- 3 cloves garlic, finely chopped
- 1-inch piece fresh ginger, grated
- 1 or 2 small fresh red or green chiles, depending on size and spiciness, such as Thai chiles, or 1 serrano chile, thinly sliced
- 4 cups vegetable broth or prepared vegetable bouillon
- One 14-ounce can coconut milk
- 2 cups red lentils
- 1 small handful fresh cilantro, stems finely chopped, leaves chopped and reserved for garnish
- ½ teaspoon kosher salt, plus more as needed
- 8 ounces kale, stemmed and finely chopped
- Juice of 2 medium limes

Heat a 4- to 6-quart saucepan over medium heat and add 1 tablespoon of the oil. Add the cumin, fennel, and turmeric and toast the spices, stirring constantly, until fragrant, about 1 minute.

Stir in the remaining 2 tablespoons oil, add the onions, and cook, stirring occasionally, until softened, 5 to 6 minutes. Add the garlic, ginger, and half of the chiles and cook, stirring frequently, for 1 minute. Remove half of the onion-chile-spice mixture and reserve it (you'll use it to garnish the finished dish).

Add the vegetable broth, coconut milk, lentils, cilantro stems, and salt to the pot. Raise the heat to medium-high and cover to bring to a gentle boil. Remove the lid, reduce the heat to medium-low, and cook, stirring occasionally, until the lentils are tender, 15 to 20 minutes. Add the kale and cook until softened, about 5 minutes. Stir in the lime juice, taste, and add more salt as needed.

Ladle the dal into individual bowls or a large serving bowl. Spoon the reserved onion mixture over the top and add the remaining sliced chiles. Garnish with the cilantro leaves and serve immediately.

WHOLE WHEAT NO-KNEAD PEASANT BREAD

It's not uncommon for someone who's only ever listened to the Grateful Dead's studio-recorded music to be a little confused the first time they listen to a live recording of deliciously lengthy musical improvisation. They might even start to get a little anxious and fidgety, not because they don't like what they're hearing, but because, if you're used to thinking you know where a song is going, and then it suddenly starts going somewhere else—somewhere totally new and uncharted—it can be a little unsettling at first. But if you know the Dead, you know they're never gonna leave you stranded. They're always going to get you someplace good by the end of the song, even if it wasn't where you originally thought you were heading. You have to trust the band—and their process—then sit back, close your eyes, and let the music take you on a journey.

YIELD: 1 LARGE LOAF

- 2⅓ cups all-purpose flour, plus more for dusting
- 1¾ cups whole wheat flour
- 1½ teaspoons kosher salt
- ⅔ teaspoon instant yeast
- 1¾ cups cool water

Combine the flours, salt, and instant yeast in a large mixing bowl. Use a whisk (or dough whisk, if you've got one) to thoroughly combine the dry ingredients.

Make a well in the center of the dough and pour in the water. Use a wooden spoon or a rubber spatula to mix the ingredients. It will look like a wet, shaggy blob. This is what we're going for.

Cover the bowl with a clean kitchen towel, plastic wrap, or a fitted lid (a pot or frying pan lid that sits on top of the bowl works well) and leave it in a draft-free spot in your kitchen (inside a turned-off microwave or on a counter away from a window are good options).

Let the dough rise for 18 to 20 hours. If your kitchen is warm, it should be ready after 18 hours. If it's on the cooler side, you'll likely need to go the full 20. The dough is ready when it has more than doubled in size and is flat and bubbly across the surface.

Flour a clean, dry workspace and carefully tip the bowl on its side. Use a rubber spatula or clean hands to very gently ease the dough onto the floured workspace. Flour your hands and the top of the dough, then fold the edges into the middle to make a ball. Carefully flip it over so the seam side is on the bottom and continue to smooth the dough and tuck the edges underneath to tighten it.

Lay a piece of parchment paper on your workspace and very carefully lift the dough ball onto it, keeping the seam side on the bottom (a bench/dough scraper or large flat spatula can help make this easier). Sprinkle the surface of the dough lightly with flour, then cover it with a clean, dry kitchen towel or a clean, large overturned mixing bowl. Let the dough rise for 1½ to 2 hours (check it after 1 hour, if your kitchen is very warm). The dough is ready when the ball has more than doubled in size.

CONTINUES

After the first hour of rising, position a rack in the middle of your oven and preheat the oven to 450°F. While the oven preheats, put a heavy 6- to 8-quart pot with an oven-safe lid (like a Dutch oven) on the middle rack.

Score the top of the loaf by running a very sharp knife across the top of it once or twice. This will release air and encourage the bread to expand even further in the oven.

Carefully remove the pot from the oven and remove the lid (keep it nearby because you will need it soon). Lift the risen, scored dough by the edges of the parchment and quickly and carefully place the loaf and parchment inside the hot pot. Immediately replace the lid and put it back in the oven.

Let the loaf bake, covered, for 30 minutes. Do not lift the lid—this will release steam and prevent the loaf from rising correctly. After 30 minutes, remove the lid and bake for 15 to 20 minutes more, until the loaf is browned and crackly on top.

After baking, lift the loaf out of the pot using the parchment paper. Transfer it to a cutting board or a cooling rack and let cool completely (at least 30 minutes and up to an hour) before slicing.

CHEDDAR-CHIVE BISCUITS

These flaky-beyond-belief, chive-studded biscuits with ribbons of tangy cheddar and bits of black pepper in every bite do not mess around. While they require a bit of effort to prepare, they are a perfect do-ahead side for a big meal, like a holiday dinner or an elaborate brunch, as the biscuits may be prepared up to 3 months in advance, frozen, and baked straight from the freezer.

Note: The biscuits call for buttermilk, which makes their crumb extra tender. You can buy it or make it. To make it, combine 1 cup whole milk or plant-based milk with 1 tablespoon lemon juice or distilled white vinegar. Stir well and let sit for 5 to 10 minutes to thicken.

YIELD: 12 BISCUITS

3½ cups all-purpose flour; a blend of all-purpose and whole wheat; or a 1:1 gluten-free all-purpose flour, plus more for dusting

2½ teaspoons baking powder

¼ teaspoon baking soda

1½ teaspoons kosher salt

2 teaspoons sugar

1 cup (2 sticks) chilled unsalted butter (dairy or plant based), cut into small cubes, plus 2 or 3 more tablespoons, melted, for brushing

1 cup shredded sharp cheddar cheese or vegan shreds (alternatively, skip the cheddar in the biscuits and serve chive-studded biscuits with a batch of Better Cheddar Vegan Cheese Dip on page 74 on the side for spreading)

1 large bunch fresh chives or 6 green onions, thinly sliced

Several grinds black pepper

1 cup buttermilk, chilled (see headnote)

Grease or line a rimmed baking sheet with parchment paper or a silicone baking mat.

In a food processor, combine the flour, baking powder, baking soda, salt, and sugar. Pulse a few times to mix, then add the cold, cubed butter. Pulse until the mixture turns to clumps the size of peas. Transfer the butter-flour mixture to a large bowl. Add the cheese, chives, and pepper to the mixture and use your hands to gently combine. Pour the buttermilk over the butter-flour mixture, stir a few times to ensure it's incorporated, then use your hands to knead it a few times until a dough forms. It will appear dry and crumbly; this is okay.

Lightly flour a clean, dry work surface and turn the mixture out onto it. Use your hands to pat the mixture into a large square about 1 inch thick.

Use a sharp knife or dough scraper to cut the square into 4 squares. Stack the squares, then gently press down on the top of the stack of squares to flatten. Cut them into 4 squares again, stack them on top of each other, and gently push down. Working quickly (handle the dough as little as possible to keep from softening the butter or overdeveloping the gluten, which will make the biscuits tough), use your hands to pat the dough into another 1-inch-thick square (it should be about 8 inches square).

Use a sharp knife to cut the dough into 12 square biscuits. Transfer the squares to the prepared baking sheet and transfer to the freezer for at least 30 minutes. If you are not planning to bake them right away, transfer the biscuits to an airtight container once they freeze solid.

Arrange a rack in the middle of the oven and preheat the oven to 425°F.

Brush the tops of the biscuits with the melted butter and put them in the oven.

After 5 minutes, reduce the heat to 400°F and continue baking for 15 to 20 minutes more, until the biscuits are golden brown and have risen.

Serve hot or at room temperature. Leftovers will keep in an airtight container in the refrigerator for 2 to 3 days. Reheat in a 300°F oven until they are warmed through.

BROCCOLI-KALE GRATIN

This gratin has all the comfort and decadence of potatoes au gratin without the wait. The process is quite similar to making baked macaroni and cheese: You boil the main ingredients (in this case, broccoli and kale rather than pasta), stir them into a cheesy sauce, top with a crunchy topping, and bake until browned and bubbly. This dish is easy to make vegan if you can get your hands on vegan cream substitute and good vegan cheese (the vegan Parmesan from Violife works well), but you may also swap the cream and cheese for a batch of Better Cheddar Vegan Cheese Dip on page 74 and reduce the baking time to 17 to 20 minutes. The finished dish will have a slightly different flavor profile, but it will still be very good.

YIELD: 4–8 SERVINGS

Kosher salt

3 cups stemmed and chopped kale (about ½ bunch Tuscan kale or 4 large leaves dinosaur kale)

2 medium heads broccoli, florets and stems chopped

1 tablespoon extra-virgin olive oil

2 cloves garlic, chopped

1 medium onion, chopped

2 cups heavy cream (or vegan heavy cream, such as those from Silk or Califia Farms)

A few pinches ground nutmeg

6 ounces sharp white cheddar cheese (dairy or plant based), shredded (about 1½ cups shredded)

A few grinds black pepper

½ cup raw almonds, chopped or crushed

Preheat the oven to 400°F.

Bring a large pot of lightly salted water to a boil over high heat and add the kale and broccoli. Reduce the heat to medium-low and cook for 4 to 5 minutes, then drain. The vegetables should be tender-crisp and retain their green color.

Heat the olive oil in a medium pot over medium heat. Add the garlic and onion and cook for 3 to 4 minutes, until very fragrant. Stir in the cream and nutmeg and continue to cook, stirring occasionally, until slightly thickened, 3 to 4 minutes. Add 4 ounces (1 cup) of the cheese, stir to melt, and season with ½ teaspoon salt and the pepper. Remove from the heat.

Stir the cooked broccoli and kale into the cheese sauce and combine well. Divide among four large or six to eight small ramekins or oven-proof bowls, or scrape into an 8-by-8-inch baking dish. Top with 2 ounces (½ cup) of cheese and a sprinkle of the almonds.

Bake for 22 to 25 minutes, until golden brown and bubbly. If desired, place under the broiler set to high for 1 to 2 minutes for a crusted top. Let cool slightly; then serve.

WHOLE WHEAT TORTILLAS/FLATBREAD

While these soft, pillowy rounds are technically tortillas, and the key to the best quesadillas and burritos should you choose to use them that way, they work equally well wherever you might serve roti, pita, naan, or any other flatbread: with soups, curries, dips, or hot out of the pan, smeared with some really good, salted butter. While yeasted flatbreads (like the ones found in Start with a Ball of Pizza Dough on page 152) are always a treat, these versatile ones come together much more quickly and help make any dish extra-special.

YIELD: 6–10 TORTILLAS OR FLATBREADS, DEPENDING ON SIZE

1 cup whole wheat flour

1 cup all-purpose flour, plus more for dusting

1½ teaspoons baking powder

½ teaspoon kosher salt

3 tablespoons extra-virgin olive oil

¾ cup hot (but not boiling) water

NOTE: If you don't have whole wheat flour on hand, these can be made entirely with all-purpose flour. If you want to make them gluten-free, use a 1:1 all-purpose gluten-free baking flour and stir the oil and 2½ tablespoons psyllium husks into the water before adding to the dry ingredients.

Whisk the flours, baking powder, and salt together in a medium mixing bowl (or use a stand mixer or food processor). Add the olive oil and use your hands, a fork, or the stand mixer or food processor to work it into the dry ingredients as thoroughly as possible.

Stream in the hot water, mixing constantly until a soft dough begins to form. Knead the dough for 4 to 5 minutes, until very soft and elastic. Let the dough rest at room temperature for at least 20 minutes (or as long as overnight in the refrigerator).

Divide the dough into 6 large, 8 medium, or 10 small pieces. Form each piece into a smooth ball. Flour a clean, dry workspace and use a rolling pin to roll the dough out as thinly as possible (the large tortillas should be 10 to 12 inches in diameter, the medium ones should be about 8 inches in diameter, and the small pieces should be 5 to 6 inches in diameter).

Heat a frying pan that is 1 or 2 inches larger than your largest dough round over high heat. Do not grease. Cook the dough rounds for 30 to 60 seconds on one side, or until bubbles appear on the uncooked side and the underside is bubbly and browned in spots. Flip and cook on the other side for about 30 seconds. It should puff up while cooking.

Repeat with the remaining dough rounds, keeping the cooked tortillas wrapped in a clean towel to keep them warm.

Serve immediately or store in an airtight container in the refrigerator for up to a week.

FIRST SET

QUICK, CASUAL ENTRÉES

If you've been to a lot of Dead shows (or listened to a lot of recorded live shows), you've likely noticed a pattern to the types of songs the band plays in the first versus the second set. A showgoer can usually count on there being something of an arc, with the first set containing shorter, often faster-paced, sometimes more lighthearted, and straightforward songs. Over the course of the night, the intensity, complexity, and length of the songs slowly ramp up, peaking about halfway through the second act, when an epic 15- to 20-minute rhythm-section improvisation begins.

This chapter is the culinary equivalent of the first set at a Dead show: You've been to the lot for a preshow grilled cheese or maybe a falafel, you entered the venue, and maybe you were even lucky enough to get to walk by the dressing rooms. You caught the opening act and got to watch the guys tune up ("Little Bunny Foo Foo" has never sounded so good). Now, finally, the house lights have gone down, and it's time for the show to get going. In other words, it's time for the main course.

Like the songs in a typical Grateful Dead first set, the entrées in this chapter are enjoyable regardless of when you consume them. (Is there ever really a bad time to listen to the Dead?) Also like the songs in the first set, they're on the casual side—unfussy, straightforward, and quick to prepare. Think weeknight meals, which require less effort but still have a high payoff, like grain bowls, veggie burgers, and tacos. These are the recipes you want to make when you're low on time, energy, or even funds but want something you'll feel grateful to be eating.

PLANTAIN-BLACK BEAN VEGGIE BURGERS

We're lucky to be living in an age where finding a delicious meat-like vegetarian burger is as easy as going to the grocery store. Unlike veggie burgers of yore, today's meat substitutes look, smell, and taste so close to the real thing that it can be hard to tell the difference. This smoky, flavorful burger, however, is different. Like commercial beef alternatives, it's savory, high in protein, and equally terrific on a bun or over lightly dressed greens. Unlike the store-bought variety, it's also rich in fiber, thanks to an entire can of black beans, complex in flavor, and significantly cheaper per serving. (Plus, you probably already have most of the ingredients in your pantry.) For a quick smoky-spicy aioli to serve with it, mix regular or vegan mayonnaise with a few spoonfuls of the adobo sauce the chipotle peppers are packed in.

YIELD: 4 SERVINGS

2 tablespoons extra-virgin olive oil, avocado oil, or grapeseed oil, plus more for the burgers

½ red onion, finely diced

½ red bell pepper, seeded and finely diced

2 cloves garlic, minced

1 canned chipotle pepper (in adobo), finely chopped

One 15-ounce can black beans, rinsed and drained

1 very ripe plantain (the peel should be blackened), diced

1 small handful fresh cilantro (about ¼ cup, loosely packed)

½ teaspoon kosher salt

Freshly ground black pepper

3 tablespoons all-purpose, whole wheat, or oat flour

4 burger buns of your choice (the nutty flavor of sprouted wheat buns works nicely), for serving

Sliced raw onion, or Quick-Pickled Onions (page 41), for serving

Sliced tomato, sliced avocado, lettuce leaves, sprouts (optional), for serving

Heat a large frying pan over medium-high heat and add 1 tablespoon of the oil. When hot, add the onion and sauté for 1 to 2 minutes, until it begins to soften. Then add the red bell pepper, garlic, and chipotle pepper and continue to cook, stirring occasionally, for another 2 minutes, until the vegetables are soft and fragrant. Transfer the cooked vegetables to a bowl to cool. Leave the pan on the stove; you'll use it to cook the burgers shortly.

In a mixing bowl, combine the black beans and plantain. Smash gently together using the back of a fork or your hands. You're not looking for a smooth paste, just a cohesive mixture. Stir it into the cooked onion-pepper mixture along with the cilantro, salt, pepper, and flour. Form the mixture into 4 patties, brush liberally with oil, and set aside.

Heat the frying pan over medium-high heat and add the remaining 1 tablespoon oil. Cook the burgers for 3 to 4 minutes on each side, or until crisp and browned.

Serve on buns with your favorite spreads and toppings.

CHIPOTLE CARROT TACOS

This vegetarian (and easily vegan-ified) taco recipe makes the humble carrot the star of the show, buoyed gorgeously by supporting actors chipotle, maple syrup, creamy queso fresco or feta, a limy vinaigrette, and a shower of fresh herbs, chiles, and pepitas to finish. Serve it with rice, beans, or cabbage slaw if you've got the bandwidth, but if not, no worries. This quick and easy taco has everything you need within it, all wrapped up in a soft corn tortilla.

YIELD: 4 SERVINGS

8 large or 10 medium carrots, ends trimmed, peeled, and cut into 1-inch chunks

1 medium yellow onion, diced

1 canned chipotle pepper, or more to taste, in adobo, finely chopped, plus a few spoonfuls of its sauce

1 tablespoon maple syrup

4 tablespoons extra-virgin olive oil

¾ teaspoon kosher salt

Several grinds black pepper

Eight 6-inch corn tortillas, blue or yellow

Juice of 1 lime

1 clove garlic, minced

4 ounces queso fresco or feta, crumbled (omit or use plant-based feta for a vegan version)

1 small handful fresh mint, chopped (about ¼ cup chopped)

1 small handful fresh cilantro, chopped (about ¼ cup chopped)

2 green onions, chopped, or Quick-Pickled Onions (page 41)

1 jalapeño, thinly sliced

Handful toasted pepitas (optional)

Preheat the oven to 375°F.

Put the carrots and onion in a large bowl and add the chipotle pepper and adobo, maple syrup, 2 tablespoons of the oil, ½ teaspoon of the salt, and pepper to taste. Toss to coat and spread on a rimmed baking sheet.

Roast for 25 to 30 minutes, stirring halfway through to ensure the vegetables brown evenly.

While the vegetables roast, wrap the tortillas in foil. When the vegetables have about 10 minutes of cooking time left, put the tortillas on a separate rack in the oven to warm them.

In a small bowl, whisk together the remaining 2 tablespoons oil, lime juice, garlic, remaining ¼ teaspoon salt, and pepper to taste. Set aside.

Remove the vegetables and the tortillas from the oven and drizzle the vegetables with the lime-oil mixture. Toss well.

To assemble the tacos, arrange the tortillas on a platter (be careful opening the foil packet—it'll be hot) and divide the carrots, queso, herbs, green onions, jalapeño, and pepitas, if using, over the top of each tortilla. Alternatively, place the tortillas, carrot mixture, and toppings on the table and let everyone assemble their own tacos. Serve immediately.

YAM AND BLACK BEAN TACOS

These healthy and filling tacos are a snap to prepare. The key to cooking sweet tubers like yams and sweet potatoes quickly on the stovetop is to cut them in a small dice (this also creates a bit more surface area for the spices to penetrate during cooking, which yields a super-flavorful finished product). Once you nail this technique, feel free to experiment with other root vegetable–bean combos: butternut squash and white beans are great together, as are Yukon gold potatoes and pintos.

YIELD: 4–6 SERVINGS

½ teaspoon kosher salt, or more to taste

½ teaspoon garlic powder

½ teaspoon onion powder

¼ teaspoon ground cumin

1 teaspoon chili powder

Eight to twelve 6-inch corn tortillas

3 tablespoons extra-virgin olive oil

1 medium onion, diced

2 large (6 to 7 inches long) red garnet yams or sweet potatoes, (preferably ones with orange flesh, but any sweet potato or yam variety will work), peeled and diced into ¾-inch cubes

Two 15-ounce cans black beans, rinsed and drained

1 cup water

2 medium avocados, peeled, halved, pitted, and sliced

1 large handful fresh cilantro, chopped (about ½ cup chopped)

Preheat the oven to 250°F.

Combine the salt, garlic and onion powders, cumin, and chili powder in a small bowl. Mix well and set next to the stove.

Wrap the tortillas in foil and place in the oven to warm while you prepare the other components of the tacos.

Heat 1 tablespoon of the olive oil in a large, heavy-bottomed frying pan over medium heat. Add the onion and cook for 3 to 4 minutes, until it begins to brown. Scrape the cooked onion into a bowl and place it next to the stove.

Add the remaining 2 tablespoons olive oil to the pan over medium heat and add the diced yams. Stir well to distribute the oil and sprinkle with the spice mixture. Stir again to distribute.

Cook, stirring occasionally, for 10 to 12 minutes, until the yams are cooked through. Watch them carefully to make sure they don't burn.

While the yams cook, put the rinsed beans in a medium pot with the water and heat over low heat. Cover the pot and turn off the heat once the beans are heated through.

To assemble the tacos, carefully remove the warm tortillas from the oven. Top each tortilla with a little bit of the yam mixture, a spoonful of beans, a spoonful of cooked onion, a couple of slices of avocado, and a pinch of cilantro. Serve immediately.

EGGLESS EGG SALAD SANDWICHES

The heyday for eggless egg salad may have been in the 1970s (many an eggless egg salad sandwich were surely served as preshow fuel for Dead Heads during that time), but it's so good, not to mention easy, healthy, and incredibly cheap to make, that it's long overdue for a comeback. This salad can also be served with crackers, over greens, or on its own.

YIELD: 4 SERVINGS

One 14-ounce package medium or firm tofu (not silken)

⅓ cup mayonnaise (regular or plant based)

2 ribs celery, finely diced

1 small or ½ medium shallot, finely diced

½ teaspoon ground turmeric

½ teaspoon cayenne pepper

1 tablespoon of your favorite mustard, or more to taste

A few dashes of your favorite hot sauce (optional)

½ teaspoon kosher salt

A few grinds black pepper

4 large or 8 smaller slices bread, preferably something sturdy and whole grain, such as Whole Wheat No-Knead Peasant Bread (page 111)

Drain the tofu and place it in a mixing bowl. Crumble it, being careful not to overwork it. You're looking for small clumps, the size of chopped hard-boiled eggs, not fine crumbs.

Gently fold in the mayonnaise, mixing well to distribute evenly. Stir in the celery, shallot, spices, mustard, hot sauce, if using, salt, and pepper to taste. Chill for at least 30 minutes.

Toast the bread if desired and divide the eggless egg salad among the slices, serving either open-faced or with a second slice on top.

NOTE: The eggless egg salad will keep for a week covered tightly in the refrigerator, so this is a great one for meal prep.

LEMONGRASS TEMPEH BANH MI

In Vietnam, banh mi, a sandwich served on a short baguette, spread with spicy mayonnaise, and often filled with pâté, roasted pork, and lots of fresh and pickled vegetables, is, in addition to being the ultimate grab-and-go meal, the country's national sandwich. This vegetarian (and vegan-possible) take on it differs slightly from most banh mi, in that it features a few slices of avocado, and in place of cooked pork, it's made with nutty, fermented tempeh cooked in a soy-and-lemongrass sauce, but the spicy mayo, quick-pickled veggies, and fresh cucumber and cilantro are all true to the classic.

YIELD: 4 SERVINGS

½ cup distilled white vinegar

2 tablespoons sugar

1½ teaspoons kosher salt

1 cup water

1 large carrot, peeled and grated or cut into matchsticks

1 small daikon (no more than 1 pound), peeled and grated or cut into matchsticks, or 1 pound red radishes, thinly sliced

2 tablespoons soy sauce, tamari, or coconut aminos

Juice of 1 lime

2 cloves garlic, minced

2 tablespoons maple syrup or honey

1-inch piece fresh ginger, minced

2 stalks fresh lemongrass, finely chopped (white part only; discard the tough parts), or 1½ tablespoons store-bought lemongrass paste

One 8-ounce package tempeh, cut into 3-inch strips

¼ cup mayonnaise (regular or plant based)

2 teaspoons sriracha, plus more for serving

2 tablespoons neutral oil, such as avocado or grapeseed oil

Four 6-inch French rolls or 1 or 2 baguettes (depending on size), cut into four 6-inch pieces

1 ripe avocado, peeled, halved, pitted, and sliced

½ English cucumber or 1 Persian cucumber, thinly sliced

1 large handful fresh cilantro

Combine the vinegar, sugar, salt, and water in a small pot over high heat. Cover and bring to a boil. Once boiling, turn off the heat, add the carrot and daikon, and cover the pot again. Let sit for 5 minutes, then transfer the contents to a heat-proof glass container, add 4 or 5 ice cubes, and refrigerate, uncovered, while you prepare the sandwiches.

Combine the soy sauce, lime juice, garlic, maple syrup, ginger, and lemongrass in a medium bowl. Whisk until incorporated. Add the sliced tempeh to the bowl and let marinate for at least 20 minutes (up to 24 hours).

While the tempeh marinates, whisk together the mayonnaise and sriracha in a small bowl. Refrigerate until ready to use.

Heat the oil in a large frying pan over medium-high heat. Remove the tempeh from the marinade and shake off the excess. Add the tempeh to the pan and cook for about 3 minutes on each side, or until golden brown and lightly crisp on the edges. Pour the remaining marinade over the top and cook, tossing to avoid scorching, until the sauce is absorbed.

To assemble the sandwiches, split each roll lengthwise, leaving the seam intact, so it opens like a book. Divide the mayonnaise mixture among the rolls, spreading it inside on both sides.

On each roll, layer one-fourth of the tempeh, a few slices of avocado, the cucumber, 2 to 3 tablespoons of the carrot-daikon mixture, and one-fourth of the cilantro. Serve the sandwiches sliced in half if desired, and pass more sriracha at the table.

NOTE: If you live near an Asian specialty market, look for banh mi tay, small baguette rolls made specifically for banh mi. Although this sandwich will work with any crusty hoagie-style roll, banh mi tay contain a bit of rice flour and no fat, giving them a light and airy texture that works beautifully with the flavors and textures of the sandwich.

MEATLESS MEATBALL SANDWICHES

Despite coming together in under 30 minutes, these hearty sandwiches taste as if they just came out of an Italian deli. Using onion and garlic powder instead of chopped onion and garlic lends concentrated, long-cooked onion and garlic flavor, which helps these meatballs taste as if they spent hours simmering in the tomato sauce. The meatballs and tomato sauce are also great on their own or served over hot pasta.

YIELD: 4 SANDWICHES

FOR THE MEATBALLS

½ cup panko breadcrumbs

½ cup water

One 1-pound package vegan ground beef, such as that from Beyond or Impossible brands

2 ounces Parmesan cheese, grated (dairy or plant based)

1 teaspoon onion powder

1 teaspoon garlic powder

¼ teaspoon dried oregano

1 large handful fresh parsley, finely chopped (about ½ cup chopped)

1 teaspoon kosher salt

A few grinds black pepper

2 tablespoons extra-virgin olive oil

FOR THE SANDWICHES

1½ cups Simple Tomato Sauce (see Start with a Pot of Tomato Sauce on page 148) or other prepared marinara sauce

Four 6-inch sturdy sub rolls, ciabatta rolls, focaccia rolls, or baguettes

¼ cup Tofu Pesto (page 53), store-bought pesto, or ½ cup lightly packed fresh basil leaves

Eight 1-ounce slices low-moisture mozzarella (dairy or plant based)

Preheat the oven to 400°F. Lightly grease a rimmed baking sheet with olive oil or line it with parchment paper or a silicone baking mat.

To make the meatballs: In a large mixing bowl, combine the breadcrumbs and water and mix well. Let rest for 10 minutes to hydrate the breadcrumbs. Add the vegan ground beef, Parmesan, onion and garlic powders, oregano, parsley, salt, and pepper. Mix well with a wooden spoon and use a cookie scoop or soup spoon to make twelve to sixteen 1½-inch balls and place them on the prepared baking sheet.

Lightly drizzle the meatballs with the olive oil and bake for 12 to 15 minutes, until nicely browned.

To make the sandwiches: While the meatballs cook, heat the tomato sauce in a large frying pan over medium heat to warm through. Add the cooked meatballs to the sauce and stir gently to coat.

Spread both sides of each roll with the tofu pesto, if using, and put 3 or 4 meatballs on the bottom half of each roll (cut the meatballs in half to fit if necessary). Spoon a little extra sauce over the top of the meatballs, then top the meatballs on each roll with 2 slices of the mozzarella. The cheese will begin to melt from the heat of the meatballs and sauce, but if you want it to melt more, place the sandwiches under the broiler briefly, just until the cheese is bubbly.

Top each sandwich with the basil, if using, and the top halves of each roll. Serve immediately.

KIND BURRITO BOWLS

This ultrasimple, flavor-loaded, rice-and-bean bowl is extremely cheap, thanks to its simple ingredients (and the magic of rice + beans = complete protein), making it a great option when you've got other purchases on your mind. But perhaps the kindest thing about this is that it requires almost no effort to put together, which makes it perfect for those nights when you just cannot be bothered to think about fixing dinner. It's especially fast once the rice is cooked. You can also make a double batch of Tomato Rice (page 105) and save half in the freezer.

YIELD: 4 SERVINGS

Two 15-ounce cans black or pinto beans, drained and rinsed

1 cup water

¼ teaspoon kosher salt

¼ teaspoon garlic powder

¼ teaspoon chili powder

⅛ teaspoon ground cumin

1 recipe Tomato Rice (page 105)

4 ounces cheddar or jack cheese (dairy or plant based), shredded, ½ cup Better Cheddar Vegan Cheese Dip (page 74), or store-bought vegan queso

1 heaping cup shredded cabbage, lettuce, or other greens of your choice

1 ripe avocado, peeled, halved, pitted, and cubed

½ medium white onion, finely diced

Hot sauce or salsa, for topping

2 tablespoons sour cream (dairy or plant based), Greek yogurt (dairy or plant based), or Cashew Crema (page 46)

1 large handful fresh cilantro, chopped (about ½ cup chopped)

Combine the beans and water in a pot over medium heat. Sprinkle with the salt, garlic powder, chili powder, and cumin and stir well to distribute. Cook the beans for 3 to 5 minutes, until heated through.

Divide the rice and beans evenly among four bowls and top with the cheese, cabbage, avocado, onion, hot sauce, sour cream, and cilantro.

MU SHU VEGGIE BOWLS

Traditional mu shu (also known as moo shoo or moo shi) is a northern Chinese dish of stir-fried meat, vegetables, and egg served in very thin crepe-like wheat pancakes. Mu shu gets its name from the pale-yellow blossoms on the osmanthus tree—said to be similar in color to the ribbons of egg. This version makes the eggs optional and offers crumbled tofu as a substitution (feel free to sprinkle ½ teaspoon of ground turmeric over the crumbled tofu to give it a similar yellow hue). It also swaps the traditional wraps for rice, making this a quick and easy weeknight meal, but if you want to stick to tradition, look for Mandarin pancakes in Asian specialty markets (or use flour tortillas) and let people fill pancakes with the vegetable mixture and pass extra hoisin at the table.

YIELD: 4 SERVINGS

3 tablespoons neutral oil, such as avocado or grapeseed oil

4 large eggs, beaten, or 8 ounces firm tofu, crumbled

¼ cup hoisin sauce, plus more for serving

3 tablespoons rice vinegar

2 teaspoons toasted sesame oil

1 tablespoon cornstarch

8 to 10 shiitake mushrooms, stems removed and caps thinly sliced

1 large carrot, grated or cut into matchsticks

½ medium green or red cabbage, cored and thinly sliced (about 4 cups sliced)

3 green onions, sliced, plus more for garnish

1 cup fresh or frozen snow peas or sugar snap peas, chopped

4 to 6 cups cooked white or brown rice

Heat a large frying pan over medium-high heat and add 1 tablespoon of the oil. Pour the eggs, if using, into the pan in a thin, even layer, as if you're making an omelet. Cover the pan and let cook for 1 to 2 minutes, checking periodically, just until firm. Once firm, remove from the heat and let cool, then slice into thin 2-inch strips. (If using tofu, cook, stirring frequently, for 2 to 3 minutes, just until it begins to take on color, then remove from the heat.)

In a small bowl, whisk together the hoisin sauce, rice vinegar, sesame oil, and cornstarch. Set aside.

Heat the same pan you cooked the eggs or tofu in over medium-high heat and add the remaining 2 tablespoons oil. Add the mushrooms and carrot and cook for 2 to 3 minutes, stirring frequently, until they begin to brown. Stir in the shredded cabbage, green onions, and snow peas and cook another 2 to 3 minutes, until the cabbage begins to wilt.

Return the cooked eggs or tofu to the pan. Raise the heat to high and pour the sauce mixture over the vegetables and eggs. Toss well to coat and cook just until the sauce has thickened slightly, about a minute.

To serve, divide the rice and vegetable mixture among four bowls. Top with sliced green onions and extra hoisin, if desired.

BLACK PEPPER TOFU AND ASPARAGUS RICE BOWLS

When it comes to crispy tofu, there are generally two paths: fry it in hot oil or bake it, coated in a bit of oil, in a hot oven. Although the final cooking step of this vegan rice bowl is done in a frying pan, the tofu gets its toothsome crunch from baking it before combining it with the asparagus and sauce. This rice bowl comes together rapidly once the tofu is out of the oven, so make sure your rice is ready for it.

YIELD: 4 SERVINGS

1 tablespoon cornstarch

3 teaspoons freshly ground black pepper

½ teaspoon kosher salt

¼ cup soy sauce, tamari, or coconut aminos

1 tablespoon maple syrup or honey (reduce to 2 teaspoons if you use coconut aminos instead of soy sauce or tamari)

2 teaspoons rice vinegar

One 16-ounce package firm or extra-firm tofu, drained, patted dry, and cut into 1-inch cubes

4 tablespoons coconut oil or neutral oil, such as avocado or grapeseed oil

1 pound asparagus, tough ends trimmed and cut into 2-inch pieces

1-inch piece fresh ginger, peeled and minced or grated

2 cloves garlic, minced

6 cups cooked white or brown jasmine rice or Coconut Rice (page 104)

3 green onions, thinly sliced

Preheat the oven to 400°F. Lightly grease or line a rimmed baking sheet with parchment paper or a silicone baking mat.

In a small bowl, mix together the cornstarch, 2 teaspoons of the pepper, and salt. In another small bowl, stir together the soy sauce, maple syrup, and rice vinegar.

Put the tofu in a medium mixing bowl and add 3 tablespoons of the oil. Use your hands or a large spoon to mix well to combine, ensuring all the tofu is well coated. Sprinkle the cornstarch mixture over the top and toss well to coat. Spread the tofu on the prepared baking sheet and bake for 10 to 12 minutes, until very crisp on the bottom. Flip the tofu pieces and cook for another 8 to 10 minutes, until crisp on the other side. Once the tofu has finished baking, let it cool on the baking sheet while you cook the asparagus.

Heat a large frying pan over medium-high heat and add the remaining 1 tablespoon oil. Add the asparagus and sauté for 2 to 3 minutes, until tender. Reduce the heat to medium, add the ginger, garlic, and remaining 1 teaspoon pepper and sauté for another 1 to 2 minutes, until very fragrant.

Add the tofu to the frying pan with the asparagus and use a wooden spoon or spatula to gently toss. Pour the soy sauce mixture over the tofu and asparagus. Cook, stirring occasionally, until the sauce has reduced and coated everything nicely, 2 to 3 minutes.

Divide the rice among four bowls and add the tofu-asparagus mixture. Top with the sliced green onions and serve immediately.

SPICY CHICKPEA CURRY

There are many preparations of korma, a dish usually consisting of meat and/or vegetables simmered in a sauce of spices, yogurt, and ground nuts originating on the Indian subcontinent. It's also the dish from which this easy vegetarian (or vegan) curry of canned chickpeas simmered in a spicy, creamy, and slightly tangy sauce takes its inspiration. Serve it over rice or with warm flatbread.

YIELD: 4–6 SERVINGS

½ cup raw cashews

2 tablespoons butter (dairy or plant based), ghee (clarified butter), or neutral oil, such as avocado or grapeseed oil

2 teaspoons garam masala

2 teaspoons yellow curry powder

2 teaspoons ground coriander

2 teaspoons chili powder (preferably Kashmiri chile powder)

1½ teaspoons ground cumin

1 medium yellow onion, chopped

3 cloves garlic, minced

1-inch piece fresh ginger, grated or minced

1 jalapeño, seeded and finely chopped (reserve a few pinches for garnish, if desired)

3 tablespoons tomato paste

One 14-ounce can coconut milk (reserve 1 tablespoon for garnish, if desired)

Three 15-ounce cans chickpeas, drained and rinsed

Juice of ½ medium lemon

Cooked rice or Whole Wheat Tortillas/Flatbread (page 117), for serving

1 large handful fresh cilantro, chopped (about ½ cup chopped)

In a medium bowl, pour boiling water over the cashews to cover. Cover the bowl with a plate or lid and let soak for at least 15 minutes.

Heat a large frying pan over medium-high heat and add the butter. Add the spices and cook, stirring frequently, just until very fragrant, about 30 seconds, then add the onion, garlic, ginger, and jalapeño. Reduce the heat to medium and cook until the onion softens and begins to brown, 3 to 4 minutes.

Add the tomato paste and cook for 1 to 2 minutes, stirring occasionally, until it begins to reduce. Remove from the heat and let cool for 5 minutes.

Drain the soaked cashews and add them to a blender with the coconut milk. Carefully scrape the contents of the pan into the blender and blend on high speed until very smooth, at least 1 to 2 minutes.

Pour the contents of the blender back into the pan, add the chickpeas, and cook over medium-high heat for 5 to 7 minutes, until everything is heated through and the sauce begins to bubble and reduce.

Remove from the heat and stir in the lemon juice. Divide the rice among four to six bowls, ladle the chickpea mixture on top, and garnish with the reserved coconut milk and jalapeño, if desired, and cilantro.

SHIITAKE RISOTTO CAKES

It's hard to beat a dish of creamy risotto with tender bits of shiitake mushrooms, fresh chives, and Parmesan that is formed into patties, dredged in crunchy panko, and pan-fried in olive oil until they turn golden and crisp. Serve them over greens, in a shallow bath of Romesco Sauce (page 43), or put them on a bun, perhaps spread with a little Vegan Green Goddess Dressing (page 47) or Tofu Pesto (page 53), and serve veggie burger style.

YIELD: 4 SERVINGS

6 cups vegetable broth or water

6 tablespoons extra-virgin olive oil, plus more as needed

8 ounces shiitake mushrooms, stems removed and caps chopped

1 medium white or yellow onion, finely diced

3 cloves garlic, minced

Pinch ground nutmeg

1½ cups uncooked arborio rice

12 fresh chives, finely chopped

1 cup grated Parmesan (dairy or plant based)

½ teaspoon kosher salt

A few grinds black pepper

¾ cup panko breadcrumbs

Pour the broth into a medium saucepan and heat over medium heat. Once heated through, reduce the heat to low and cover the pan.

In a large heavy-bottomed saucepan over medium heat, heat 2 tablespoons of the olive oil. Add the shiitakes and sauté just until they begin to brown, 3 to 4 minutes. Add the onion and garlic and sauté for 3 to 4 minutes, until they are translucent and very fragrant. Add the nutmeg and stir well.

Add 2 more tablespoons of olive oil, then add the rice to the pot, stir well to coat it with the oil, and sauté for 2 minutes to lightly toast the rice. Add the warm broth ½ cup at a time, stirring after each addition, allowing the rice mixture to cook until most of the liquid has absorbed before adding the next measure.

Once all the liquid has been absorbed, remove from the heat and stir in the chives, ⅔ cup of the Parmesan, salt, and pepper. Taste and adjust the seasoning if necessary.

Scrape the mixture onto a rimmed baking sheet or large casserole dish and flatten with a rubber spatula. Refrigerate for 30 minutes. Once the mixture is very cold, remove it from the refrigerator.

Heat the remaining 2 tablespoons olive oil in a large frying pan over medium-high heat. Pour the panko and remaining ⅓ cup Parmesan into a shallow bowl and mix well. Set the bowl next to the frying pan.

Use an ice cream scoop or a large spoon to scoop up about ¼ cup of the chilled risotto mixture. Form it into a 4-inch-wide patty and dredge on both sides in the panko-Parmesan mixture, patting gently to help it adhere. Place the risotto cake into the hot oil and cook for 2 to 3 minutes on each side, until golden brown and crispy.

CURRIED PUMPKIN PIZZAS

Homemade pizza might not sound like a good solution for nights when you need a quick and easy dinner, but you'd be surprised. When you have a batch of pizza dough (see Start with a Ball of Pizza Dough on page 152) in the fridge (or a pound of dough from your local grocery store or pizzeria), pizza night is, in addition to being a lot of fun for everyone making and eating it, a snap to throw together. This unique pie breaks many rules of traditional pizza, swapping tomato sauce for one made of canned pumpkin (*not* to be confused with pumpkin pie filling, which is sweetened and would not taste good here), cheddar for the usual mozzarella, and finishing with a drizzle of Leafy Green Relish (page 38), Quick-Pickled Onions (page 41), and toasted sesame seeds. The recipe can easily be scaled up or down, and it also works well on a charcoal or gas grill. To grill the pizzas, cook each round of dough without any toppings for 2 to 3 minutes, then flip, top, and cook, covered, until the cheese melts and the crust is crisp, 5 to 7 minutes.

YIELD: FOUR 10-INCH PIZZAS

1 cup canned 100% pure pumpkin purée

1 teaspoon curry powder

½ teaspoon kosher salt

A few grinds black pepper

All-purpose flour, for dusting

1 pound homemade pizza dough (page 152) or store-bought pizza dough

Fine cornmeal, for sprinkling the pizza peel (or use flour)

8 ounces cheddar cheese, shredded (2 cups shredded)

4 to 8 tablespoons Leafy Green Relish (page 38), or more to taste

4 teaspoons toasted sesame seeds (optional)

¼ cup Quick-Pickled Onions (page 41)

Preheat the oven to 550°F (or as high as it will go). Arrange a rack in the lowest part of the oven. Place a pizza stone, pizza steel, or overturned baking sheet on the rack and let it preheat with the oven for at least 30 minutes.

In a mixing bowl, combine the pumpkin, curry powder, salt, and pepper. Mix well.

On a lightly floured work surface, divide the pizza dough into 4 equal pieces. Roll each piece into a smooth ball. Use your hands (not a rolling pin, which will make the dough tough) to stretch the ball into a 10-inch circle.

Sprinkle a pizza peel or a second overturned baking sheet with cornmeal (or lightly flour it) and place the dough round on it. Spread the dough with ⅙ cup of the pumpkin mixture (it should be a very thin layer), leaving a ½-inch border for the crust. Top the pumpkin with 2 ounces (½ cup) of the shredded cheese.

Position the pizza peel or pan over the preheated pizza stone, pointing toward the back, and slowly, carefully slide the pizza off the peel so it's sitting directly on the pizza stone.

Cook for 8 to 10 minutes, rotating the pie with a spatula halfway through cooking, until the crust is nicely browned and the cheese is bubbly and slightly browned. If you want more browning on the cheese, place it under the broiler on high heat for a minute or two.

If you want to serve the pizzas as they finish cooking, proceed to the next step, then repeat the process with the remaining pizzas. If you prefer to serve them all at once, assemble and bake the rest of the pizzas, then reduce the oven to 400°F and place all the cooked pizzas directly on the oven racks to stay warm (it's okay if they are not spaced perfectly evenly—you're just trying to heat them before serving).

To finish the pizzas, drizzle each one with 1 to 2 tablespoons of the green relish, sprinkle a teaspoon of the sesame seeds over the top, and distribute a few pickled onions across the pie. Slice and serve hot.

RIFF BREAK

IMPROVISATIONAL COOKING

Perhaps one of the best-known and well-loved moments of a Dead show takes place a bit into the second set. It is, for many people, the most intense moment of the night—a 15- to 20-minute improvisational percussion.

Riffing, jamming, and creating brand-new music in the moment is the Dead's signature style, spinning beautiful chaos into pure magic on any given show night.

Although it may seem to have been manifested out of thin air, the band's musical synergy is the result of extremely hard work, practice, dedication, near-obsessive fine-tuning—in other words, a lot of preparation. Musical chemistry doesn't just happen—you can't fly to the moon by the seat of your pants unless you have really, really good pants.

Much about cooking can be learned from the way the Dead honed their improvisational skills, and if you're a seasoned cook, you'll likely recognize this logic: Really good food—some of the best food you've ever made—can happen when you trust your intuition and learn to cook on the fly, but you've got to be organized.

The first step is to make sure you have a decently stocked pantry. The second step is to practice—a lot. Embrace recipes and cook them as they're written until you feel confident that you understand the dish inside and out. Then start to look for components you can tweak according to your preferences. Many of the Dead's songs contain parts with an open musical structure. This was intentional, a space created for improvisation. You'll find similar spaces in the recipes in this book too, headnotes encouraging you to try recipes with your favorite vegetable/grain/legume. Once you're confident with a recipe, it's time to experiment. Taste as you go. Get in touch with what you like—and don't like—but learn to trust your intuition. The more you cook (and eat!), the better you'll get at being able to look at a pile of raw ingredients and immediately see the path to something delicious.

There are only six recipes in this chapter and each one is very basic: simple ways to cook a pot of rice, a pot of tomato sauce, a pot of noodles, a tray of roasted potatoes, a block of tofu, and a ball of pizza dough. None is a complete meal by itself, though. For that, your creativity is required. Even when the Dead improvised long sections of a song, the first line or two are played as written. In the same way, the recipes in this chapter are merely a starting point. They include prompts and suggestions to get you started, but the precise path from basic recipe to finished dish is up to you.

START WITH A TRAY OF ROASTED POTATOES

These ultracrispy, flavorful roasted potatoes are good alongside any main course, but with the tiniest bit of additional effort, they can become the main event.

YIELD: 4–6 SERVINGS

Kosher salt

4 large or 6 to 8 medium russet or Yukon gold potatoes, scrubbed clean (no need to peel) and cut into roughly 1-inch cubes

¼ cup extra-virgin olive oil or neutral oil, such as avocado or grapeseed oil

1 teaspoon onion powder

1 teaspoon garlic powder

A few grinds black pepper

Preheat the oven to 450°F.

Fill a 4- to 6-quart pot about halfway with water and bring to a boil over high heat. Once boiling, add 2 or 3 large pinches of salt and the potatoes. Reduce the heat to medium to bring down to a simmer, then cook for about 8 minutes, or until the potatoes are still firm but tender enough to easily cut into.

Drain the potatoes and transfer them to a large mixing bowl. Drizzle with the oil and toss well to coat. Add the onion powder, garlic powder, salt to taste (start with ½ teaspoon and add more as needed), and pepper.

Transfer the potatoes to a rimmed baking sheet and arrange so they are not touching each other. Bake for 15 minutes. They should be very crisp on one side. Flip the potatoes and cook on the other side for 15 to 25 minutes (check periodically to avoid burning after 15 minutes and flip again if necessary). The cooked potatoes should be crisp on the outside and tender inside.

Let cool in the pan for at least 5 minutes to crisp them further. Serve or use in one of the following riffs.

RIFFS

POTATO TACOS AKA TACOS DE PAPA

For this addictively good but very easy-to-make taco, fill warmed corn tortillas with the roasted potatoes and top with a generous portion of shredded cheese (cheddar, jack, pepper jack, mozzarella, Better Cheddar Vegan Cheese Dip, page 74, or store-bought vegan queso), dairy or plant based—whatever you have on hand. For soft tacos, serve immediately with any taco toppings you like—for example, hot sauce, guacamole, sour cream or Cashew Crema (page 46), cilantro, minced onion. For crispy tacos, arrange the tacos on a greased rimmed baking sheet, brush them with neutral oil, and bake in a 425°F oven for 12 to 15 minutes, until the tortillas turn crispy and the cheese is melted and bubbly. Top as desired.

PESTO POTATOES WITH BROCCOLI

Combine the potatoes and 3 cups steamed or roasted broccoli florets in a large serving bowl. Add 3 to 5 tablespoons Tofu Pesto (page 53) or store-bought pesto to coat everything. Serve as is or add cubed buffalo mozzarella or diced roasted red peppers.

VEGGIE SAUSAGE, KALE, AND POTATO SKILLET

Slice as many vegetarian sausages as you want to serve into 2-inch slices. Pan-fry in a large skillet with 1 sliced yellow onion and a few cloves of chopped garlic. Add a bunch of chopped, stemmed kale leaves and cook until softened. Fold in the potatoes and serve with any sauce you like, such as Vegan Green Goddess Dressing (page 47) or Leafy Green Relish (page 38).

START WITH A POT OF RICE

This is a basic, no-fail stovetop rice recipe, but you can cook 1½ cups long- or medium-grain rice any way you like (check the package for guidance). Feel free to use other cooking grains if you like. Barley, groats, and farro all work with the riffs on the next page.

YIELD: 3 CUPS COOKED RICE

1½ cups long-grain white rice, rinsed well

3 cups water

¼ teaspoon kosher salt

Combine the rice, water, and salt in a medium saucepan over high heat and cover. Bring to a boil, then reduce the heat to low.

Simmer with the pot covered on low heat until the water is absorbed, about 18 minutes. Do not lift the lid—you want the steam to stay in the pot.

Once the rice is cooked, turn off the heat and let the rice rest, covered, for 10 minutes. This is the key to fluffy rice. Fluff the cooked rice with a fork and it's ready to use.

RIFFS

FRIED RICE

Sauté chopped garlic and ginger in a couple tablespoons of neutral oil, then add the cooked, cooled rice, breaking it up with a spoon. Continue to fry until the rice begins to crisp, then season with soy sauce, sriracha, and sesame oil. Add cooked cubed tofu (see page 147) and/or scramble in a couple of eggs, if you like. Add any chopped vegetables you've got (e.g., shredded carrots, fresh or frozen green peas, bok choy, corn kernels or baby corn, snow peas, thinly sliced cabbage) plus 3 or 4 thinly sliced green onions. Taste as you cook, adding more soy sauce, sriracha, or any other seasonings you like (white pepper is also good here). Top with more green onions and black pepper and serve.

MUJADDARA

Cook 2 thinly sliced medium yellow onions in at least 3 tablespoons olive oil until very soft and nicely browned, 6 to 8 minutes. Then add 4 or 5 cloves chopped garlic and cook until soft, 1 minute. Stir in a bit of ground cumin (¼ to ½ teaspoon) and toast until fragrant. Then add the rice and 1 to 2 cups cooked brown or green lentils. Stir well, making sure to coat the rice and lentils with the oil. Season with salt and pepper to taste. Garnish with lots of fresh cilantro and sliced green onions and serve in bowls topped with plain yogurt, if desired (dairy or plant based), and a big drizzle of something spicy, such as Leafy Green Relish (page 38) zhoug (Yemenite hot sauce made with cilantro and parsley), cilantro chutney, jarred harissa, sriracha, Spicy-Crunchy Chili Oil (page 40), or anything else you like.

CRISPY RICE

Preheat the oven to 400°F. Grease a rimmed baking sheet with 2 tablespoons neutral oil. Pat the cooked, cooled rice into a flat rectangle shape on the pan and drizzle the top with a bit more oil (another tablespoon or two). Bake for 10 minutes, until it starts to get brown and crispy. Then break the rice up with a spoon and return the pan to the oven for another 10 minutes. Continue baking in 5- to 10-minute intervals, until the rice is crispy and brown throughout. (This is a recipe where it's ideal to check the pan a lot during cooking.) Once the rice is crispy and browned throughout, remove it from the oven to cool. It's perfect in a simple salad of greens and protein and particularly good in Sesame Slaw with Peanuts on page 90, as well as Mango-Avocado Salad on page 94. Add it to scrambled eggs or tofu, or even roll it into sushi for tempura-like crunch.

START WITH A POT OF PASTA

You want a long-strand pasta here, ideally one that is wheat based. It's also fine to use something gluten-free just make sure it acts as much as possible like conventional pasta after cooking—that is, it does not get mushy and fall apart after being cooked.

YIELD: 6–8 SERVINGS

1 pound dried long-strand pasta, such as spaghetti or fettuccine

Cook the pasta or noodles in a large pot of salted boiling water for the time indicated on the package. Reserve 1 cup of the cooking water, if necessary (check out the riffs that follow to determine this). Drain the pasta (do not rinse, unless you want to serve the pasta cold per the riffs that follow).

RIFFS

PASTA AND SAUCE

In a large frying pan or pot, toss the hot pasta with any fresh or jarred sauce you like (good options are Tomato Sauce, page 148; Tofu Pesto, page 53; and Romesco Sauce, page 43) over medium heat until heated through. Add a drizzle of extra-virgin olive oil or a couple pats of butter (dairy or plant based) and toss well. Garnish with grated Parmesan, chopped fresh herbs like parsley or basil, a pinch of kosher salt, and freshly ground black pepper.

GARLICKY BUTTER NOODLES WITH PARM

Sauté lots of thinly sliced garlic and red pepper flakes in unsalted butter (dairy or plant based) or olive oil in a large frying pan over medium heat just until the edges begin to brown, then add the warm pasta and toss thoroughly to coat. Continue tossing over medium heat and add the pasta water a little at a time, along with grated (not shredded) Parmesan cheese (dairy or plant based, like the kind from Violife), a couple of tablespoons at a time. Continue tossing until a light, creamy sauce forms. Serve the hot, sauced pasta under a shower of chopped fresh parsley, more Parmesan, and more red pepper flakes, if desired.

SPICY-CRUNCHY CHILI OIL NOODLES

Toss hot noodles in as much Spicy-Crunchy Chili Oil (page 40) or store-bought chili crisp as you like, then season with kosher salt or soy sauce or tamari to taste. Serve as is or add toasted, chopped nuts, like peanuts or almonds, toasted sesame seeds, chopped fresh cilantro and/or green onions, and any vegetables or protein, such as crispy cubes of tofu or tempeh.

COLD PEANUT NOODLE SALAD

Rinse the noodles after cooking to cool them and remove the starch. Then toss with Peanut Sauce (page 45). Optionally, chill for 20 to 30 minutes for a colder salad. Top with cucumbers, carrots, red bell peppers, or any other firm, crisp vegetable cut into matchsticks, or cubed crispy tofu, if desired. Garnish with fresh cilantro or green onions and toasted unsweetened coconut.

START WITH A BLOCK OF TOFU

If you have anyone in your life who claims to not like tofu, you can be sure it's because they've never eaten it cooked this way. Several other recipes in this book use these crispy cubes of delicious soy protein (Buffalo Tofu, page 56, Chicken(less) Pho, page 84, and Mango-Avocado Salad, page 94, for example), but there are many more that will benefit from them.

YIELD: 4 SERVINGS

One 16-ounce package firm or extra-firm tofu

2 to 3 tablespoons neutral oil, such as avocado or grapeseed oil

Kosher salt

Wrap the tofu block in a clean kitchen towel and gently pat it dry. Cut the tofu into ¾-inch pieces.

Heat the oil in a large frying pan over medium-high heat. Add the tofu to the pan, salt it well, and let cook, undisturbed, for 4 to 5 minutes (check after 4 to minutes make sure it's not burning), until a thick, golden-brown crust develops. Use a spatula or wooden spoon to flip the tofu as best you can and cook at least one other side until it is also golden brown and crispy.

Drain on a paper towel or a cooling rack to remove any excess oil.

RIFFS

TOFU TACOS OR BURRITOS

Add the tofu cubes to any taco or burrito recipe in this book to add a hefty dose of protein and crispy texture. You could also toss the cubes in the Shortcut Mole Sauce (see Start with a Pot of Tomato Sauce, page 148) on page 149, along with any cooked vegetables you have on hand. Roasted mushrooms or sweet potatoes are good, as are the roasted potatoes on page 142. Garnish with your favorite taco toppings and dig in.

TOFU LETTUCE CUPS

Sauté garlic, ginger, sliced green onions, and red pepper flakes in a couple tablespoons of neutral oil in a large frying pan over medium-high heat. Add ½ cup chopped mushrooms (shiitakes are nice) and ⅓ cup drained, chopped canned water chestnuts. Cook everything until it's nicely browned and add the tofu. Drizzle with hoisin sauce, soy sauce, or tamari; a few dashes of rice vinegar; and a drizzle of toasted sesame oil. Stir well to combine everything and top with toasted sesame seeds. Put the pan on the table with a big pile of butter lettuce leaves (at least 10) and let everyone assemble their own lettuce cups at the table. Bonus: Adding the Crispy Rice (see Start with a Pot of Rice, page 144) on page 145 gives this unbelievable crunchy texture.

CRISPY TOFU SUMMER ROLLS

Add the crispy cubes to the Vegetable Summer Rolls on page 69. Roll up tightly and serve with Peanut Sauce (page 45).

START WITH A POT OF TOMATO SAUCE

Generally, when you cook tomato sauce with a clear plan for its ultimate use (layered in lasagna, say, or spooned over eggplant Parm), the usual approach is to add a lot of aromatics, like herbs or spices, to build distinct flavor from the start. Here, the approach to flavor building is also intentional, but in a different way. The idea here is to make a good but simple tomato sauce that tastes of long-cooked tomatoes, a hint of garlic, and just a touch of heat from the red pepper flakes, which can serve as a blank canvas for a variety of dishes with lots of different flavor profiles.

YIELD: ABOUT 5 CUPS

¼ cup extra-virgin olive oil

4 cloves garlic, thinly sliced

½ teaspoon red pepper flakes, or more to taste

Two 28-ounce cans crushed tomatoes

½ teaspoon kosher salt, or more to taste

A few grinds black pepper

1 bay leaf

Heat a large, heavy-bottomed pot over medium heat, then add the olive oil. Add the garlic and cook just until it begins to take on color, 30 to 60 seconds. Add the red pepper flakes and stir well to combine. Stir in the crushed tomatoes, salt, pepper, and bay leaf.

Cover the pot and raise the heat to medium-high to bring the sauce to a low boil, then reduce the heat to low and simmer with the pot covered until the sauce has thickened, 25 to 35 minutes.

Turn off the heat and discard the bay leaf. Taste for seasoning and adjust as needed.

RIFFS

QUICK TOMATO SOUP

Heat some or all of the sauce (depending on how many people you're feeding) over medium-high heat and thin it out to your desired consistency using vegetable broth, water, or a combination. Add any herbs or spices you like, such as more garlic and fresh basil for classic tomato soup. If you want to add cream, use heavy cream, plant-based heavy cream, or a handful of cashews that have been soaked and puréed. For a totally different take, add fresh chiles, grated ginger, 5 or 6 makrut lime leaves, and coconut milk for Cambodian tomato soup. Serve with grilled cheese or flatbread and a green salad or slaw.

PANEER, TOFU, OR CHICKPEA TIKKA MASALA

Heat a couple of tablespoons of unsalted butter (dairy or plant based), neutral oil, or ghee (clarified butter) in a large, heavy-bottomed pot over medium heat. Then add 1 teaspoon smoked paprika (or Kashmiri chile powder, if you can find it) and 1 teaspoon garam masala. Add a finely chopped onion, 2 or 3 cloves minced garlic, and a small (1-inch or so) piece fresh ginger, grated. Cook together until the onion is lightly browned and softened. Then pour in 2 cups tomato sauce (or more if desired). Add salt to taste. Cover the pot, reduce the heat to low, and simmer for 25 to 30 minutes. Purée the sauce in a blender or food processor or using an immersion blender, adding a little water to thin as needed. Stir in ⅓ to ½ cup heavy cream, depending on your desired level of creaminess. For a vegan sauce, add a handful of soaked cashews when you purée the sauce or use coconut milk. Taste again and adjust the seasoning as needed. Then add 16 ounces cubed paneer or extra-firm tofu or one or two 14-ounce cans drained, rinsed chickpeas. Cook until everything is warmed through and serve with basmati rice or flatbread, fresh cilantro, and Leafy Green Relish (page 38), if desired.

SHORTCUT MOLE SAUCE

Heat a couple tablespoons of oil in a medium, heavy-bottomed pot over medium heat and add a couple garlic cloves, 1 to 2 teaspoons chili powder, ¼ teaspoon ground cumin, a pinch of ground cinnamon, and a couple pinches of dried oregano. Add 2 tablespoons all-purpose flour (gluten-free 1:1 flour works just fine) and whisk constantly for 2 or 3 minutes to make a roux. Add 1 cup vegetable broth or prepared bouillon and 1 cup tomato sauce. Add a tablespoon of smooth peanut butter (or other nut butter), 1 or 2 teaspoons apple cider vinegar, a handful of dark chocolate chips (or 1 to 2 ounces chopped dark chocolate), and salt to taste. Spoon the sauce over tacos or nachos; use in burritos or in place of enchilada sauce; as a sauce for cooked, crumbled vegan beef to make the best Sloppy Joes of your life; or as a sauce for any cooked beans, vegetables, and/or vegetarian proteins you have on hand, ideally wrapped in warm corn or flour tortillas.

START WITH A BALL OF PIZZA DOUGH

When you're short on energy, time, and meal ideas, a baking project might not seem like a sensible solution. But a big batch of fresh pizza dough is a gift not only to the lucky people at your dinner table but also to your future self. In addition to being full of nutrient-dense, flavorful ingredients, truly effortless to make (you combine some simple ingredients in a bowl, give them a stir, then ignore them for the better part of a day), and extremely difficult to mess up, this recipe makes *a lot* of dough. This means that when it has risen and is ready to go, you'll have enough for a night of pizza, with plenty left over. Of course, in the event that you didn't make pizza dough 12 hours before thinking about what to make for dinner, all of the riffs can be made with store-bought dough.

YIELD: 1 POUND PIZZA DOUGH

1½ cups whole wheat flour

1⅔ cups all-purpose flour, plus more for dusting

⅔ teaspoon instant yeast

1½ teaspoons kosher salt

1 tablespoon flaxseed meal

1 tablespoon hemp hearts

1 tablespoon sesame seeds

1⅔ cups cold water

Olive oil, as needed

In a large bowl, whisk the flours, yeast, salt, flaxseed meal, hemp hearts, and sesame seeds until thoroughly combined. Add the water and mix well until a shaggy dough forms. Don't worry about how it looks now.

Cover the bowl with a clean kitchen towel, plastic wrap, or a fitted lid and allow to rise for at least 12 hours (and up to 20), until it has more than doubled. If your kitchen is very warm, it will likely be ready after 12 hours. If it's cooler, rising will take closer to 20 hours.

When the dough has risen, flour a flat surface and gently turn the dough out onto the flour. Use a knife or bench scraper to divide the dough into 4 to 6 equal pieces. Gently shape the pieces into balls by pulling the ends toward the center and rolling gently. Place each ball you aren't using into an airtight container, lightly oil it, and cover tightly. Refrigerate for up to a week or freeze for up to 3 months. When ready to use, place it on the counter and allow it to come to room temperature for 2 to 3 hours.

RIFFS

DIY PIZZA NIGHT

The Curried Pumpkin Pizzas on page 138 are a great place to start. One you get the basic technique down, experiment with your own sauces. There are several in this book to get you started, such as the sauce in Start with a Pot of Tomato Sauce (page 148), Tofu Pesto (page 53), Romesco Sauce (page 43), or even Vegan Ranch (page 48). Top with cheese (dairy or plant based) and bake as directed in the pumpkin pizza recipe. Use the recipe's suggested fillings, or let your imagination run wild.

FLATBREAD

Divide the dough into 6 to 8 small pieces and roll into tight balls on a lightly floured surface. Heat a large, heavy-bottomed frying pan (preferably not a nonstick one) over medium-high heat and cook the rounds in the dry frying pan until browned on one side and bubbly on the other side. Flip and cook the other side until the dough round starts to puff a bit. Repeat with the remaining dough balls. The flatbread can be used in any recipe that calls for pita (such as the Kind Shawarma-Spiced Cauliflower Burritos on page 21, or the Baked Hemp Falafel on page 27), or naan (like the Coconut-Kale Red Lentil Dal on page 109 or the Kind Broccoli Stem Soup on page 81). You can even wrap your favorite salad in a big piece of flatbread. Eat it at home or wrap tightly in foil and take it with you.

ROLLS AND/OR BREADSTICKS

Nearly any yeasted bread can be made from this dough. Twist the dough into 6-inch snakes, let rest, covered, until they puff up a bit, about 20 minutes, bake at 450°F for 12 to 14 minutes, until golden brown, and then brush with butter and a sprinkle of garlic salt. These make fresh breadsticks that go perfectly with any soup or salad or the Better Cheddar Vegan Cheese Dip on page 74. Or roll into balls, tuck into an oiled baking dish, let them rest, covered, for 20 to 30 minutes, until puffy, then bake for 22 to 25 minutes at 375°F and serve with salted butter or olive oil.

SECOND SET

DEEPER, MORE COMPLEX (BUT NOT COMPLICATED!) ENTRÉES

If the first set of a Grateful Dead show establishes a groove—tight, focused, and on the familiar side—the second set is where the band lets loose. While the first set has moments of energy and excitement, it is structured and grounded, focused more on familiar hits, grounding the audience in something comfortable and accessible. The energy in the first set is lighter, giving everyone a chance to settle in before the long-distance climb of the second set's invited improvisation, spontaneity, and deeper, more immersive experience begins.

Second set songs are often longer, with extended jams that wander into uncharted territory, seamlessly blending into one another. This set is often more spontaneous and less predictable. It's about taking risks, exploring new musical landscapes, and creating a one-of-a-kind experience.

The same shift happens in the kitchen with this chapter. The entrée recipes in the First Set chapter are a bit more approachable, familiar, and casual, designed to get you into a rhythm in the kitchen and feed you well in a timely manner and without too much fanfare. Here, while the recipes are still doable for cooks of any skill set, some of them might be a little bit off the beaten path or a little more complex. Just as the songs in the second set of a Dead show stretch out and take on new forms, these recipes invite you to slow down and dive deeper into the joys of cooking (and tasting).

These dishes might require a bit more patience, some unexpected ingredients, or a little more need to trust the process, but I encourage you to embrace the challenge of cooking new foods. The whole experience is meant to be savored and enjoyed, and like the band's most memorable jams, the payoff and the journey are one and the same.

CAST-IRON BIBIMBAP

Bibimbap, a Korean dish of rice; cooked, raw, and pickled vegetables; and a variety of proteins, such as chicken, beef, seafood, and eggs; all topped with a spicy fermented chili sauce, is traditionally served in a hot stone pot known as a *dolsot*. This pot serves not only to hold the contents of the dish but also to crisp the rice continuously as you eat it. If you don't have a *dolsot* at home, you an get an effect similar to that of the *dolsot* from a heavy-bottomed cast-iron pan, which retains heat much as the *dolsot* does and will also crisp the rice beautifully. If you don't have a cast-iron pan, use another large, heavy-bottomed pan or pot and let it sit on the heat a bit longer to crisp the rice.

YIELD:
3–4 SERVINGS

⅓ cup gochujang

One 16-ounce package extra-firm tofu or plant-based chicken, such as the kind made from vital wheat gluten, cut into 2-inch strips

5 tablespoons neutral oil, such as avocado or grapeseed oil

16 ounces fresh baby spinach or 8 ounces frozen spinach

4 cloves garlic, chopped

Kosher salt and freshly ground black pepper

2 to 4 large eggs (omit for a vegan version)

3 cups cooked medium-grain brown or white rice

1 tablespoon toasted sesame seeds

2 carrots, peeled and sliced into thin ribbons with a peeler or shredded

4 green onions, chopped

Kimchi, for serving

In a medium bowl, whisk the gochujang paste with enough water to make it pourable (3 to 4 tablespoons should do the trick). Transfer half of the thinned gochujang to a small bowl and set aside.

Add the tofu to the thinned gochujang in the medium bowl and toss to coat evenly.

Heat a large (12- to 15-inch) cast-iron pan over medium heat and add 1 tablespoon of the oil. Add the tofu and cook for 2 to 3 minutes per side, until it browns and the gochujang thickens.

Remove the cooked tofu from the pan and transfer it to a plate. Shut off the heat and carefully wipe out the pan using a wet paper towel or kitchen towel. No need to get it perfectly clean; you're just trying to remove any charred bits.

Turn the heat on to medium-high and add a second tablespoon of oil to the pan. Add the spinach and garlic and stir well to combine. Cook just until the spinach is hot and the garlic is softened, about 5 minutes. Season to taste with salt and pepper. Scrape the spinach into a medium bowl and set aside.

If using eggs, heat 1 tablespoon of oil in the cast-iron pan. Fry the eggs to your desired doneness and transfer to a clean plate.

Add the remaining 2 tablespoons oil to the pan over medium-high heat. Lightly wet your hands (this prevents sticking) and carefully pat the rice into the hot pan, taking care not to touch the pan itself with your fingers (this may also be done with a rubber spatula or large spoon). Let the rice cook in the pan for 3 to 4 minutes, just until it begins to get crispy on the bottom.

Remove the pan from the heat and arrange the toppings on the rice. Drizzle the reserved thinned gochujang over the top. Finish with the toasted sesame seeds, carrots, green onions, and kimchi.

RED CURRY WITH SWEET POTATO AND TOFU

Could you, theoretically, make this spicy, creamy, dreamy Thai curry with store-bought red curry paste? Sure. But it would not be as intensely flavored, vibrantly red, and fragrant. And making it with store-bought curry paste would not leave you with the pride of having made curry paste from scratch—not to mention the adrenaline of having handled hot chiles in the service of your dinner.

YIELD: 4 SERVINGS

FOR THE RED CURRY PASTE

3 large dried red New Mexico chiles

10 small dried chiles de árbol

2 medium shallots or 1 medium red onion, chopped

12 to 15 cloves garlic, chopped

1-inch piece fresh ginger, chopped

1-inch piece galangal, chopped (if you can't find galangal, use another 1-inch piece fresh ginger)

1 tablespoon ground coriander

1 teaspoon ground cumin

½ teaspoon kosher salt

FOR THE CURRY

Two 15-ounce cans coconut milk

1 to 2 tablespoons maple syrup or honey

1 tablespoon soy sauce or tamari

Several grinds black pepper

2 cups vegetable broth or prepared bouillon

3 medium sweet potatoes or yams, 1-inch cubed, unpeeled

One 12-ounce package firm tofu, 1-inch cubed, drained, patted dry

1 red onion, quartered

3 cloves garlic, chopped

1 head broccoli, cut into florets

1 medium red bell pepper, seeded and cut into 1-inch chunks

FOR SERVING

Cooked rice or Coconut Rice (page 104)

1 jalapeño, thinly sliced (optional)

1 large handful fresh cilantro, chopped (about ½ cup chopped)

To make the curry paste: Remove the stems and seeds from the dried chiles. Chop the chiles into small pieces and soak them in a bowl of hot water for 10 minutes to soften. Drain. (Be sure to wash your hands very well with hot water and soap after handling the chiles.)

Put the soaked chiles, shallots, garlic, ginger, galangal, coriander, cumin, and salt in a food processor or blender and purée into a paste, scraping down the sides as needed.

Store the unused curry paste in an airtight container in the refrigerator for up to 3 months.

To make the curry: In a medium, heavy-bottomed pot over medium-high heat, whisk together 1 to 2 tablespoons (depending on heat tolerance) of the curry paste and the coconut milk. Add the maple syrup to taste, plus the soy sauce and pepper. Stir well and add the vegetable broth.

Reduce the heat to medium and add the sweet potatoes. Cook, covered, for 10 to 12 minutes, until the sweet potatoes begin to soften, and then add the tofu, onion, garlic, broccoli florets, and bell pepper. Stir gently to incorporate. Reduce the heat to medium-low, cover the pot, and cook for 12 to 15 minutes, or until the sweet potatoes yield easily to a fork and the broccoli and bell pepper are tender but not mushy.

Serve over rice and garnish with the jalapeño slices, if using, and cilantro.

NOTE: If you want to serve this with Coconut Rice (page 104), start cooking the rice just before you get going on the curry paste, and it'll all be ready to eat at the same time.

HAND-ROLLED PASTA

Who says fresh pasta requires fancy equipment? This simple recipe is in keeping with the message of gratitude and abundance the Dead and Dead Heads are known for: You already have what you need, so use it! This simple, delicious pasta requires nothing more than three extremely basic ingredients you most certainly have in your pantry and refrigerator and can be easily made.

YIELD: 4 SERVINGS

2 cups all-purpose or whole wheat flour, plus more for rolling and dusting

¼ teaspoon kosher salt

1 large egg, lightly beaten (or use ½ cup plus 2 tablespoons lukewarm water)

Put the flour and salt in a mixing bowl and stir to combine. Make a well in the flour and crack the egg into it (or pour the water in). Use a fork to gently combine the ingredients until a sticky dough forms.

If the dough is too dry, add a few drops of water until it holds together (you may not need it). Knead for about 2 minutes on a dry, floured surface until smooth and elastic. Place the dough in a bowl (the one you mixed it in is fine), cover with a clean kitchen towel, and let it rest (not in the refrigerator) for at least 30 minutes (and as much as 24 hours).

After the dough has rested, use a sharp knife to cut it into 5 or 6 equal strips. Use a rolling pin to roll each piece as thin as possible. Keep the dough and the rolling pin well-floured and keep the rolled-out dough dusted with flour.

Roll each dough strip into a loose coil. Use a sharp knife to cut the coils into 1-inch pieces (or smaller, if you want to make thinner pasta). Repeat with the remaining dough strips.

Gently unroll the coils. Cook in salted, boiling water for about 3 minutes, or until tender.

Drain and serve with your favorite sauce (such as the tomato sauce on page 148, Tofu Pesto on page 53, or Romesco Sauce on page 43).

PUMPKIN-KALE LASAGNA

Think of this lasagna as the baked pasta equivalent of a Dead song that bridges the faster-paced first set songs to the longer, more intense ones in the second set. Because, while there's no getting around the fact that lasagna *is* an involved process, this recipe is quite a bit simpler than most, thanks to time-saving no-boil noodles and only one sauce that needs to be cooked in advance. On the other hand, if you're in the mood for a project, make a double batch of Hand-Rolled Pasta (page 160) and cut into 7-by-3-inch rectangles. Parboil for 60 seconds, drain, and use in place of the no-boil noodles.

YIELD: 6–8 SERVINGS

- Two 15-ounce cans 100% pure pumpkin purée
- 2 large eggs (omit for a vegan version)
- ¼ teaspoon cayenne pepper
- 1 teaspoon kosher salt
- A few grinds black pepper
- 2 tablespoons extra-virgin olive oil
- 1 large bunch curly or lacinato/dinosaur kale stemmed and, leaves chopped
- 4 cloves garlic, minced
- ½ teaspoon red pepper flakes
- 3 tablespoons unsalted butter (dairy or plant based)
- 3 tablespoons all-purpose flour
- 3 cups whole milk (or unsweetened, unflavored almond, cashew, or soy milk)
- 1 tablespoon finely chopped fresh sage or ½ teaspoon dried sage
- ⅛ teaspoon ground nutmeg
- 10 ounces grated low-moisture mozzarella cheese (dairy or plant based; about 2½ cups grated)
- ½ cup grated Parmesan cheese (dairy or plant based)
- 1 pound no-boil lasagna noodles
- Chopped fresh parsley, for garnish

Preheat the oven to 350°F. Lightly grease a 9-by-13-inch baking dish with olive oil.

In medium bowl, whisk together the pumpkin, eggs, cayenne, ½ teaspoon of the salt, and a few grinds black pepper. Set aside.

Heat a large, heavy-bottomed pot over medium-high heat and add the olive oil and kale (in batches, if necessary) and cook for 1 to 2 minutes, until it begins to wilt. Reduce the heat to medium and stir in the garlic and red pepper flakes, then cook for 2 to 3 minutes, or until the kale is wilted. Remove from the heat.

In a medium pot over medium heat, melt the butter. Whisk in the flour to make a thick paste. Cook for 1 minute, whisking constantly. Continue to whisk while slowly adding the milk. Cook for 6 to 8 minutes, or until slightly thickened, whisking constantly (it's fine to take breaks to give your arm a rest!). Remove the bechamel sauce from the heat; stir in the sage, nutmeg, remaining ½ teaspoon salt, and a few grinds of black pepper. Set aside.

Combine ½ cup of the mozzarella and 2 tablespoons of the Parmesan in a bowl and set aside.

Pour about half of the bechamel in the bottom of the prepared dish. Add a layer of noodles, then spread the noodles with half of the pumpkin mixture. Add another layer of noodles, followed by half of the remaining mozzarella and all the remaining Parmesan. Add all of the cooked kale followed by another layer of noodles.

Spread the noodles with the remaining pumpkin mixture and remaining mozzarella. Add one last layer of noodles and pour the remaining sauce over the top. Sprinkle with the reserved mozzarella and Parmesan.

Lightly grease a sheet of foil with olive oil (or cooking spray), then cover the pan tightly with the foil, greased side down, and bake for 45 minutes. Remove the foil and bake for 15 to 25 minutes, or until the cheese is bubbly and browned in spots.

Let the lasagna rest for at least 15 minutes, cut into squares, and serve hot, garnished with parsley.

CURRIED VEGETABLE POT PIE

Pot pie is one of those dishes that is so warm and comforting, so soothing and familiar, that at first glance, you might think this is merely a vegetarian version of the frozen chicken pot pies you ate growing up. But take a peek beneath the pastry draped over your ramekin, and you'll see freshly cooked veggies, happily swimming in a creamy curry sauce. The intoxicating aroma greets you just before you take your first bite.

YIELD: 4 SERVINGS

½ cup plus 2 tablespoons all-purpose or whole wheat pastry flour

¼ cup cold butter (dairy or plant based), cut into small pieces

½ teaspoon kosher salt, or more to taste

2 tablespoons ice water

2 russet potatoes, scrubbed and diced (no need to peel)

1 tablespoons olive oil

4 cloves garlic, minced

1 onion, diced

3 fresh sage leaves, chopped

1 teaspoon curry powder

1 teaspoon chili powder, more or less to taste

¼ teaspoon ground cumin

¼ teaspoon ground coriander

3 carrots, peeled and diced

½ cup frozen green peas

½ cup heavy cream (plant-based heavy cream or full-fat coconut milk for a vegan version)

A few grinds black pepper

1 large egg or 1 tablespoon melted plant-based butter

In a food processor, combine ½ cup of the flour, the butter, and a pinch of salt. Pulse until the mixture resembles small peas. Slowly stream in the ice water with the machine running and pulse just until the dough comes together (you may need slightly more or less water—just pay attention to the dough). Remove the dough from the machine, form it into a ball, dust it lightly with flour, place it in a bowl, and immediately refrigerate for 15 minutes.

While the dough chills, bring a pot of lightly salted water to a boil over high heat and add the potatoes. Reduce the heat to medium and simmer for 10 minutes, or until a fork easily pierces the potatoes. Drain and set aside.

Heat the olive oil in a large frying pan over medium-high heat. Cook the garlic, onion, spices, and sage until fragrant, 2 to 3 minutes. Add the carrots, peas, and cooked potatoes. Stir gently.

Preheat the oven to 400°F.

In a bowl or measuring cup, whisk the heavy cream and remaining 2 tablespoons flour until combined and add it to the pan. Stir to combine. The vegetables should now be cooking in a fragrant, creamy sauce. Cook for 2 to 3 minutes, stirring occasionally. Season to taste with the salt and several grinds of pepper (about ½ teaspoon). Remove from the heat. Divide the mixture among four ovenproof bowls or ramekins or pour it all into an 8-inch pie pan and allow to cool to room temperature.

Cut the chilled dough into 4 pieces and roll each one out on a floured surface into a 5- to 6-inch circle (or a circle as large as your ovenproof bowls). Roll the dough into an 8-inch circle if you are making one big pot pie.

CONTINUES

Drape the dough over each bowl or the large pie and cut a slit in the middle to allow steam to escape.

If using the egg, beat it together with 2 tablespoons water and use a pastry brush to brush over the dough (alternatively, brush the melted plant-based butter over the top of the dough).

Bake the pot pies for 25 to 30 minutes, until the pastry is golden brown. Let cool for 5 minutes before serving.

BUTTERNUT SQUASH GREEN CHILE ENCHILADAS

Butternut squash and leafy green chard may not be the most traditional fillings for enchiladas, but if you make this recipe, you'll likely find they're right at home tucked into soft corn tortillas, filled with a green chile sauce and smothered in gooey cheese. The enchiladas are also excellent prepared with the Shortcut Mole Sauce (see Start with a Pot of Tomato Sauce, page 148) on page 149.

YIELD: 4 SERVINGS

2 medium yellow onions, diced

1 large butternut squash, peeled, seeded, and diced

3 tablespoons extra-virgin olive oil

4 cloves garlic, finely chopped

¼ teaspoon ground cumin

½ teaspoon smoked paprika

½ teaspoon kosher salt

A few grinds black pepper

1 large bunch Swiss, red, or rainbow chard, stemmed and thinly sliced

12 corn tortillas

Two 16-ounce cans green chile enchilada sauce

12 ounces jack or cheddar cheese (dairy or plant based), shredded

1 large handful fresh cilantro leaves, chopped (about ½ cup chopped)

Preheat the oven to 375°F. Lightly grease a 9-by-13-inch baking dish with olive oil and set aside.

Spread the onions and squash on a large, rimmed baking sheet and toss with the olive oil. Season with the garlic, spices, salt, and pepper and toss well to mix. Roast for 25 minutes, stirring once, until the squash is nicely browned.

Layer the chard on top of the squash and onions and return to the oven for 5 to 7 minutes to allow it to wilt. Remove the baking sheet from the oven and transfer the squash-onion-chard mixture to a bowl.

Warm the tortillas in the microwave or in a dry frying pan to soften them enough to be pliable.

Pour the enchilada sauce into a mixing bowl or baking dish. Dip a tortilla into the sauce and pull it out, shaking off excess sauce. Lay the tortilla on a flat surface. Place 2 to 3 tablespoons of butternut-chard filling and a generous sprinkle of cheese in the center of the tortilla and roll it up. Place the rolled-up tortilla, seam side down, in the prepared pan. Repeat with the remaining tortillas, sauce, filling, and cheese, reserving about ½ cup cheese for the top. Pour the remaining sauce over all the rolled tortillas in the pan and top with the reserved cheese.

Bake for 30 to 35 minutes, or until the cheese is bubbly and browned. Serve hot, garnished with cilantro.

ROASTED MUSHROOM STEAKS WITH PAN GRAVY

Mushroom steaks? As a main course? Really? *Really*, really. Searing thick, meaty mushrooms, then cooking them in a supercharged umami-laden sauce in the style of an expensive steak results in a dish that feels fancy enough to have a high price tag on the thick, cream-colored menu of a high-end steakhouse. It's fairly easy to make, but it does require you to resolve not to go poking and prodding the mushroom steak as it cooks, lest you disturb the development of the divine texture and flavor it's on its way to acquiring.

YIELD: 4 SERVINGS

¼ cup soy sauce, tamari, or coconut aminos (if using coconut aminos, omit the maple syrup or honey)

4 cloves garlic, smashed

A few grinds black pepper

1 tablespoon maple syrup or honey

½ cup water

3 tablespoons extra-virgin olive oil, plus more for cooking

1 tablespoon unsalted butter (dairy or plant based)

4 very large (7 to 9 inches) or 8 medium (4 to 6 inches) king oyster mushrooms, halved lengthwise

1 small handful fresh parsley, chopped (about 2 tablespoons chopped)

¼ cup vegetable stock, vermouth, or other wine (red or white—whatever you've got)

Stir together the soy sauce, garlic, pepper, maple syrup, water, and 2 tablespoons of the oil in a wide, shallow dish. Place the mushrooms in the dish, flat side down. Cover the dish and let the mushrooms marinate at room temperature for 30 minutes.

Heat the remaining 1 tablespoon oil and the butter in a large, heavy-bottomed frying pan over medium-high heat.

Remove the mushrooms from the marinade and shake off the excess. Reserve half of the marinade.

Place the mushrooms, flat side down, in the pan and reduce the heat to medium-low. Cook for 10 to 12 minutes, until very brown. Flip the mushrooms and let them cook for another 5 to 7 minutes on the other side. Add the reserved marinade to the pan and cook until it is almost completely absorbed.

Remove the mushrooms from the pan and top with the parsley. Add the broth to the pan and cook, scraping the browned bits off the pan, to make a pan sauce.

Once the sauce has thickened (about 1 minute), pour it over the mushrooms and serve warm.

LEMON PAPPARDELLE WITH TOASTED ALMONDS

If you've been cooking plant based for some time, you are likely familiar with the wizardry of puréed soaked cashews turning into something akin to heavy cream after a spin in the blender. However, the cashew flavor can be an issue in dishes where it isn't especially welcome (e.g., in a pasta dish). This dish, however, has the solution to that problem built into the recipe: an onion cooked in vegetable broth and puréed into the sauce, turning it supple and sweet. The onion reinforces the sauce's creamy texture and enhances the beautiful deep flavor while simultaneously masking the cashew flavor. A hit of lemon juice and sprinkle of zest brightens the dish.

YIELD: 4 SERVINGS

½ cup raw cashews

1 medium onion, diced

2 cups vegetable broth

3 cloves garlic, chopped

Zest and juice of 1 lemon, plus more zest for garnish

½ teaspoon kosher salt, or more to taste

A few grinds black pepper

1 tablespoon nutritional yeast, or more to taste

One 16-ounce package pappardelle, fresh or dried (if you can't find pappardelle, use fettucine, linguine, or any other wide, long-strand pasta, such as the Hand-Rolled Pasta on page 160)

2 tablespoons chopped, toasted almonds

A handful fresh parsley, finely chopped (about ¼ cup chopped)

Put the cashews in a small bowl and cover with boiling water. Cover the bowl with a lid or clean kitchen towel and let it sit for at least 15 minutes. Drain.

Combine the onion and 1½ cups of the broth in a large frying pan and cook over medium heat, stirring continuously, for 7 to 8 minutes, until the broth has been absorbed and the onion is very soft. Add the garlic to the pan and cook for another 2 to 3 minutes, until fragrant and translucent.

Add the soaked cashews, remaining ½ cup vegetable broth, cooked onion and garlic, lemon zest and juice, salt, pepper, and nutritional yeast to a blender. Process on high speed for 2 to 3 minutes, until very smooth and creamy. Taste and adjust the seasoning as needed.

Bring a large pot of salted water to a boil over high heat and cook the pappardelle according to the package instructions. Reserve ½ cup of the cooking water. Drain and return the pappardelle to the pot. Pour in the sauce (if you prefer your pasta to be lightly sauced, don't pour it all in).

Turn the heat to medium-low and gently toss the pasta and sauce together, adding a bit of the pasta cooking water, if necessary, to reach the desired sauce consistency. Divide the pasta among four bowls and top each one with a sprinkling of almonds, parsley, and more pepper, if desired.

BASIL RICOTTA DUMPLINGS IN ROMESCO SAUCE

Like the Hand-Rolled Pasta on page 160, this recipe is proof that fresh pasta is more within reach than you might think. Think of these ricotta dumplings—also known as *gnudi*—as large, pillowy gnocchi except they are much, much easier to make. They're made with ricotta rather than traditional potato, which can be finicky to work with and tricky to shape. If you use dairy ricotta, choose the best kind you can afford and be sure to drain any extra liquid before using it. For a vegan version, the almond-based ricotta from Kite Hill works nicely.

YIELD: 4 SERVINGS

1 cup all-purpose flour, plus more for dredging and for the plate

One 16-ounce container ricotta (whole milk dairy or plant based)

2 cloves garlic, minced

1 large handful fresh basil leaves, finely chopped (about ¼ cup chopped), plus more for garnish

1 large egg plus 2 large egg yolks, beaten together in a bowl (use a commercial egg replacer for a vegan version)

½ teaspoon kosher salt

½ teaspoon freshly ground black pepper

¼ cup grated Parmesan cheese (dairy or plant based), plus more for garnish

1½ cups Romesco Sauce (page 43)

In a large bowl, stir together the flour, ricotta, half the minced garlic, basil, egg and egg yolks, salt, pepper, and Parmesan. Continue stirring until a sticky dough forms.

Lightly flour a large platter or a baking sheet and make sure your hands are well floured as well. Keep a small bowl of flour nearby; you'll need it to continue flouring your hands. Scoop up about 1 heaping tablespoon of the dough and roll it gently in your floured hands a few times to form a smooth ball. Set the ball on the prepared platter. Repeat with the remaining dough. Set the platter aside (or refrigerate if you want to cook the dumplings later).

Warm the Romesco sauce in a small pot over low heat. Keep covered until ready to use.

Bring a large pot of salted water to a boil over high heat. Cook the dumplings, working in batches (I did it in thirds), for about 5 minutes, until they float. Remove with a slotted spoon and transfer to a large bowl.

To serve the dumplings, divide the sauce among four plates or bowls and top with the dumplings. Garnish with Parmesan and more basil.

ENCORE

DESSERTS

These days, encores are standard at most concerts. The show ends, the crowd cheers, and then, almost like clockwork, the artist(s) return(s) to the stage. But the Grateful Dead don't subscribe to that model of show-closing ending. There are many nights when, often, at the close of the second set, the band says goodnight and the show is over.

But occasionally, the band does come back and we get the ultimate treat: one more song, where the audience is lucky enough to get one more performance after thinking the magical evening has ended. The rare Dead show encore is more than just a bonus song—it's a shared celebration between band and audience, a moment where the lines separating them become blurred. They provide one final, joyful chapter to the evening, a collective acknowledgment of the special journey everyone has taken together.

When you serve dessert at the end of a meal, whether for a group of twenty or a party of one, you conjure that same sense of thrill. *Oh! I thought we were all done! But look, there's more, and it's delicious!*

Typical encores at a Dead show range from upbeat, high-energy closers to longer, slower, more exploratory ones. Similarly, the desserts in this chapter range from quick, simple, and crazy-satisfying to a bit more elaborate and intense. They may take a bit more planning and time, but they are sure to halt conversation at the dinner table as your guests take their first bite and are bombarded by intense flavor that is somehow both familiar yet unlike anything they've ever tasted before.

BANANA-COCONUT SPRING ROLLS

These crispy cylinders of ripe bananas surrounded by sweet coconut and an impromptu caramel-like sauce that forms during cooking are an elegant dessert. They are fancy enough to be served at the end of a nice meal, but also easy enough to be thrown together well after guests have arrived. They're especially good served with a scoop of green tea ice cream or lime sorbet.

YIELD: 8 SPRING ROLLS

2 ripe bananas

8 large egg roll wrappers (wrapper sizes vary among brands, but you're looking for something 6½ to 8 inches square)

4 tablespoons shredded or flaked sweetened coconut

4 tablespoons brown or coconut sugar

Ground cinnamon, for sprinkling

Neutral oil, such as avocado or grapeseed oil, for frying

Slice each banana into fourths lengthwise so you have 8 long pieces of banana. Slice the long pieces in half so you have 16 short, thin pieces of banana.

Lay an egg roll wrapper on a clean, dry surface. Make a little mound on it with 1 tablespoon of coconut and 1 tablespoon of brown sugar in the center of the wrap. Lay 2 banana slices on top of the mound, sprinkle a dash of cinnamon on the banana, and roll up, tucking in the ends of the wrapper, as though making a little burrito. Repeat with the remaining egg roll wrappers and filling ingredients.

Heat about 1 inch of oil in a medium frying pan over medium-high heat. Cook the rolls for 1 to 2 minutes on each side, until golden brown and crisp. Drain on paper towels or a cooling rack.

Serve sliced on the bias, garnished with a little more cinnamon.

PEACH HAND PIES

You know what's better than a thick slice of summer-ripe peach pie? Your very own pie—one you don't have to share with anyone (unless, of course, you want to). The crust comes together quickly, especially if you've got a food processor, but the pies are nearly as good (and even easier to make) with thawed frozen store-bought butter-based or vegan pie dough (look for the kind that comes rolled up in a cylinder rather than pressed into an aluminum pie tin). Make these in the summer, when peaches are at their sweetest and juiciest. Off-season, swap the fresh peaches for frozen, or use thinly sliced apples, berries, or any other fruit you like. Serve plain, with whipped cream, or with a scoop of vanilla ice cream.

YIELD: 4 HAND PIES

FOR THE CRUST

2 cups all-purpose flour or whole wheat pastry flour, plus more for rolling

1 cup (2 sticks) cold unsalted butter (dairy or plant based), cut into small cubes

1 large pinch kosher salt

3 to 4 tablespoons ice water

FOR THE FILLING

1 pound (3 or 4 medium) fresh white or yellow peaches, skin on, pitted and sliced

Juice of 1 lemon

¼ cup granulated or coconut sugar

Pinch kosher salt

FOR FINISHING THE CRUST

1 large egg, lightly beaten (for vegan pies, replace the egg with 2 tablespoons maple syrup diluted with a bit of water)

2 tablespoons turbinado sugar

To make the crust: Put the flour, butter, and salt in a food processor (or a mixing bowl). Pulse until the mixture looks like coarse sand. If you're working by hand, use your hands to work the ingredients together until the mixture looks like pea-size clumps.

Stream in the water, 1 tablespoon at a time, just until the mixture starts sticking to itself.

Lightly flour a work surface and tip the dough onto it. With lightly floured hands, pat it into a circle about 6 inches in diameter. Wrap the dough tightly in plastic wrap and refrigerate for at least 1 hour. You may also freeze it for up to 2 months. When you're ready to use your frozen dough, defrost it in the refrigerator overnight.

Preheat the oven to 375°F. Line a baking sheet with parchment paper, a silicone baking mat, or a light sprinkling of flour and set aside.

To make the filling: Combine the peaches, lemon juice, granulated sugar, and salt in a bowl. Stir gently to combine and let sit for 20 minutes.

Lightly flour a work surface and place the chilled piecrust on it. Roll the piecrust out until it is about ⅛ inch thick. Use a 6-inch bowl or dough cutter to punch out 4 circles. If necessary, reroll the scraps and punch again. Arrange one-fourth of the peaches in the center of a dough round, leaving a 2-inch border. Gently fold the border of dough over the peaches to make a loosely decorative edge. Transfer the pie to the prepared baking sheet. Repeat with the rest of the dough and peaches.

To finish the crust: Use a pastry brush to lightly coat each pie's crust with egg. Sprinkle the top and edges of each pie with the turbinado sugar.

Bake the pies for 25 to 30 minutes, or until the crust is golden brown and the peach filling is bubbly. Let cool slightly.

BROWN BUTTER-SPELT CHOCOLATE CHIP COOKIES

These cookies are straight-up nutty, from the toasty browned butter and the slightly sweet spelt flour, which is lighter than whole wheat flour but coarser than white all-purpose flour, making it a perfect compromise when you want flour with flavor, but not so much that it overpowers the classic chocolate chip cookie flavors here. And finally, there are the nuts, which are, well, nutty too.

YIELD: SIXTEEN 4-INCH COOKIES

1 cup (2 sticks) unsalted butter (dairy or plant based—see Note), at room temperature

1½ cups all-purpose flour

1½ cups spelt flour

1 teaspoon baking powder

½ teaspoon baking soda

1 teaspoon kosher salt

1⅓ cups packed coconut or dark brown sugar

⅓ cup granulated sugar

2 large eggs (use flax eggs, see page 12, or commercial egg replacer for a vegan version)

1 teaspoon vanilla extract or paste

1 cup semisweet or dark chocolate chips or chunks, plus more for topping (substitute nondairy chips for a vegan version)

⅓ cup raw walnuts or pecans, roughly chopped (optional)

Flaky sea salt, for finishing

NOTE: Most plant-based butters don't brown well (Miyoko's and Kite Hill are the exceptions). If your plant-based butter doesn't brown when you cook it as instructed, add 1 to 2 teaspoons smooth, mild-tasting nut butter (cashew and almond butter work well) to the pot in the first step. The fat solids from the nut butter will toast and yield results similar in flavor and texture to brown butter.

Melt one stick of the butter in a medium saucepan over medium-high heat (if you have a light-colored pan, use it here, as this will help you see clearly when the butter begins to brown). Turn the heat down to medium and cook for 5 to 8 minutes, stirring constantly, scraping any browned bits from the bottom of the pan with a wooden spoon, whisk, or spatula. The butter will foam, sizzle, and eventually brown and smell nutty. Watch it carefully, as burned butter has an unpleasant bitter flavor.

Whisk the flours, baking powder, baking soda, and salt together in a large bowl and set aside. Using a stand mixer with a paddle attachment or electric beaters, beat the brown butter, remaining 1 stick butter, and sugars in a mixing bowl until creamy, about 30 seconds. Add the eggs one at a time, beating thoroughly to ensure they are well combined. Add the vanilla and mix again.

Mix the reserved dry ingredients into the butter and egg mixture until just combined, and then fold in the chocolate chips and walnuts, if using.

Line a baking sheet with parchment paper or a silicone baking mat. Use a cookie scoop or spoon to scoop the dough into sixteen 3-tablespoon balls and arrange on the prepared baking sheet. Top each dough ball with a few chocolate chips and a small pinch of flaky salt.

Chill the dough in the refrigerator for at least 1 hour or up to 24 hours. There is no need to cover the baking sheet. Alternatively, you can freeze the dough for up to 3 months before baking (freeze until solid on the baking sheet, then transfer the frozen dough balls to an airtight container). The recipe will still work if you bake the cookies without chilling the dough first, but the flavor and texture won't be quite as developed.

Preheat the oven to 350°F.

Arrange the chilled dough balls with at least 3 inches between them (you'll need to work in batches).

Bake the cookies for 9 to 11 minutes, until the tops turn golden brown, the edges are crisp, and the centers are slightly gooey. They may appear a bit underdone, but once cool enough to eat, they'll be perfect. Let cool on the baking sheet or on a wire rack before serving.

AVOCADO BROWNIES

The reason to make these brownies has absolutely nothing to do with the fact that instead of the usual butter or vegetable oil, they're made with ripe, heart-healthy avocado, flavonoid-rich dark chocolate, and no refined sugar. Those are merely the cherries on top (or, shall we say, brownie points?) of this recipe. The reason to make these brownies is that in addition to being naturally vegan and gluten-free, making them an ideal dessert for accommodating a variety of dietary restrictions, they are the platonic ideal of a brownie: ultra rich, fudgy, and moist.

YIELD: 8 SERVINGS

½ cup blanched almond flour (not almond meal)

½ cup unsweetened cocoa powder

1 teaspoon instant espresso powder (optional but recommended)

½ teaspoon kosher salt

½ teaspoon baking soda

1 large ripe avocado, peeled, halved, and pitted

½ cup maple syrup or honey

2 large eggs (use flax eggs, see page 12, or commercial egg replacer for a vegan version)

1 teaspoon vanilla extract or paste

¼ cup dark or semisweet chocolate chips or chunks, plus more for topping (substitute nondairy chips for a vegan version)

Flaky salt, for finishing (optional but recommended)

Preheat the oven to 350°F. Lightly grease an 8-by-8-inch pan.

In a medium bowl, whisk together the almond flour, cocoa powder, espresso powder, if using, salt, and baking soda. In a blender or food processor, combine the avocado, maple syrup, eggs, and vanilla.

Add the dry ingredients to the blender or food processor and pulse until smooth. Stir in the chocolate chips. Pour the batter into the prepared pan, sprinkle a few more chocolate chips over the top of the batter, and sprinkle with flaky salt, if using.

Bake for 22 to 25 minutes, until the top is smooth and glossy and a knife or toothpick inserted into the center comes out clean. Let cool for at least 15 minutes before using a sharp knife to cut the brownies into 8 squares. Serve warm or at room temperature.

DESSERT QUESADILLAS

If you love French dessert crepes but don't want to bother with tending to finicky batter and carefully flipping ultrathin pancakes, these will get the job done in a fraction of the time and with far less effort. Think of these fillings as merely suggestions to get you started. Get creative with flavor combinations: chocolate-hazelnut spread, sliced strawberries, and whipped cream (or whipped coconut cream); a drizzle of nut butter, sliced bananas, and a touch of honey or maple syrup; or sliced mango, toasted sesame seeds, and a drizzle of sweetened, condensed milk (dairy or coconut based) are excellent combinations.

YIELD: 4 SERVINGS

Four 8-inch flour tortillas (store bought or Whole Wheat Tortillas/Flatbread on page 117)

4 ounces cream cheese (dairy or plant based), at room temperature

4 ounces dark, semisweet, or milk chocolate chips, chunks, or disks

A few dashes ground cinnamon

A few dashes kosher salt

3 to 4 tablespoons unsalted butter (dairy or plant based), plus more as needed

Confectioners' sugar, for finishing

Spread each tortilla with 2 tablespoons of the cream cheese. Sprinkle the chocolate pieces over half of the tortilla, on top of the cream cheese. Top with a dash each of cinnamon and salt, and fold over to make a half-moon.

Heat 1½ teaspoons of the butter in a medium frying pan over medium heat and cook one quesadilla on both sides, until the chocolate is melted and the tortilla is golden brown—3 to 5 minutes on each side. Don't rush it; a low-and-slow cook is necessary for a buttery, crispy exterior.

Serve immediately or transfer to a rimmed baking sheet and keep warm in a 200°F oven until ready to serve. Continue cooking the remaining quesadillas, adding more butter before each. Cut into wedges, garnish with a dusting of confectioners' sugar, and serve.

CARROT-CARDAMOM LOAF CAKE WITH CREAM CHEESE GLAZE

Between March and October 1974, the Dead toured with a sound system coined the Wall of Sound. At the time, it was the largest concert sound system ever built. It featured 48 amps and 604 speakers—each of which carried the sound of just one instrument or vocalist, which meant the sound was unprecedentedly clear. The audience was quite literally surrounded by a wall of distinct, maximized sound, making every note the band played a full-body experience for the listener. This turned-up rendition of a carrot cake takes the same approach—intensifying the whole experience by magnifying one ingredient: carrots. Roasting the carrots until deeply caramelized, then puréeing, distills their flavor far more than grating them raw, as in traditional carrot cakes.

YIELD: 6–8 SERVINGS

FOR THE CARROT PURÉE

7 or 8 medium carrots, peeled and cut into 1-inch pieces

2 tablespoons avocado or grapeseed oil, or melted coconut oil

FOR THE LOAF CAKE

½ cup avocado or grapeseed oil, melted coconut oil, or melted unsalted butter (dairy or plant based), plus more for the pan

3 large eggs (use flax eggs, see page 12, or vegan egg replacer for a vegan version)

1¼ cups granulated or coconut sugar

2 tablespoons milk (dairy or plant based) or water

1½ teaspoons baking powder

¾ teaspoon baking soda

¾ teaspoon fine sea or table salt

¾ teaspoon ground cardamom

½ teaspoon ground cinnamon

¼ teaspoon ground nutmeg

2 teaspoons grated fresh ginger or ¼ teaspoon ground ginger

2⅔ cups all-purpose flour (for a denser, nuttier crumb, replace 1 cup all-purpose flour with whole wheat or spelt flour)

½ cup chopped raw walnuts (optional), plus 1 to 2 tablespoons for garnish (optional)

¼ cup raisins (golden raisins or chopped dates also work well)

Preheat the oven to 375°F.

To make the carrot purée: Spread the carrots on a rimmed baking sheet and drizzle the oil over them. Use your hands to toss them well, ensuring each carrot is well coated. Roast for 25 to 30 minutes, until the carrots are very soft and browned.

Remove the carrots from the oven and let sit until cool enough to handle. Transfer to a food processor and purée until very smooth. Set aside until ready to use.

To make the cake: Oil, butter, or spray with cooking spray a 6-cup/8½-inch loaf pan and dust lightly with flour.

In a large bowl, whisk together the puréed carrot, oil, eggs, granulated sugar, and milk until smooth. Sprinkle the baking powder, baking soda, salt, cardamom, cinnamon, nutmeg, and ginger over the batter and whisk until well combined. Fold in the flour, just until mixed, then fold in the walnuts, if using, and raisins. Scrape the batter into the prepared loaf pan.

Bake the loaf for 60 to 65 minutes, until domed and browned. A cake tester or toothpick should come out clean when inserted into the center.

CONTINUES

FOR THE CREAM CHEESE GLAZE

4 ounces cream cheese (dairy or plant based), at room temperature

½ cup confectioners' sugar, sifted

1 teaspoon vanilla extract or paste

3 to 4 tablespoons milk (dairy or plant based)

To make the glaze: In a stand mixer or bowl with a handheld mixer, beat the cream cheese until very creamy. Gradually beat in the confectioners' sugar and vanilla, then beat in 3 tablespoons of the milk, or a bit more as needed to make the glaze loose enough to drizzle.

Refrigerate if not ready to use. The glaze will thicken the longer it sits in the refrigerator and will loosen after sitting out for a few minutes. You may also add a tablespoon of milk (dairy or plant based) to thin it enough to pour over the top of the cake.

Let the cake cool in the pan, then gently remove it and transfer to a platter or plate. Don't try to glaze the cake while it's hot—the glaze won't stick.

Pour the glaze over the top of the cooled cake and use an offset spatula or rubber scraper to gently spread it over the top, allowing it to drip down. It's important to make sure the cake has cooled fully before icing; otherwise, the glaze will melt too much. If desired, top with a light sprinkle of finely chopped walnuts. Slice and serve. Leftovers may be stored in the refrigerator for up to a week.

VEGAN PUMPKIN CHEESECAKE

If you've ever stood before a picked-over holiday dessert table filled with half-eaten, sad-looking grocery store pies, sighed, then made yourself a cup of decaf and slumped back to your seat, you need this pie recipe. Whether you're vegan or not, this perfectly spiced, creamy chilled cheesecake will be the hit of any holiday table. Better yet, neither the crust nor the filling requires baking.

YIELD: 6–8 SERVINGS

FOR THE FILLING

1½ cups raw cashews

2 tablespoons apple cider vinegar

¼ cup coconut cream (not coconut milk)

2 tablespoons neutral oil, such as avocado or grapeseed oil

½ cup maple syrup, coconut sugar, or brown sugar

⅓ cup canned 100% pure pumpkin purée

½ teaspoon kosher salt

¼ teaspoon ground nutmeg

½ teaspoon ground cinnamon

Pinch ground cloves

1½ teaspoons vanilla, dark rum, or whiskey (note that the filling is not cooked, so the flavor of these will be stronger than when cooked in a pie, and although it is a very small amount, any alcohol content will be present)

FOR THE CRUST

1½ cups raw pecans

1 cup pitted Medjool dates

¼ teaspoon kosher salt

Dash ground cinnamon

Optional toppings: whipped cream, whipped coconut cream, ground cinnamon, freshly grated nutmeg, fresh pomegranate seeds

To make the filling: Place the cashews in a bowl, cover with hot water, cover the bowl with a fitted lid or clean kitchen towel, and let soak for at least 15 minutes.

To make the crust: Place all the crust ingredients in a food processor and pulse until the mixture resembles a crumbly dough and sticks together when a clump is pinched.

Line a 9-inch springform pan with parchment paper. Wet your hands in cool water and press the crust into the bottom of the springform pan to completely cover it.

To continue the filling: Drain the cashews, then purée in a blender or food processor along with the remaining filling ingredients until very smooth and creamy (let the machine run for at least 2 minutes). Pour the filling into the crust-lined pan and smooth with an offset spatula or scraper.

Freeze for 6 to 8 hours (preferably overnight), until the filling is very firm.

Let thaw in the refrigerator, then slice and serve cold. It's delicious plain or add a dash or two of cinnamon or freshly grated nutmeg, top with whipped dairy or coconut cream, or a handful of fresh pomegranate seeds.

NOTE: If you want to make a vanilla (or another flavor) cheesecake, omit the pumpkin, increase the coconut cream to ⅔ cup, and use any other flavorings you like. A swirl of melted chocolate, lemon curd, or raspberry jam are all good options.

FROZEN FIG MILKSHAKES

Date shakes, first made famous in the United States by the Valerie Jean Date Shop at a historic date orchard in Palm Springs, but popularized throughout the region, get a lot of recognition, but these sweet and creamy, naturally vegan shakes, made from frozen fresh (rather than dried) figs and almond or coconut milk deserve your attention. They're also the perfect solution to figs' tendency to ripen faster than it's possible to eat them. As soon as the figs you brought home from the farmers' market begin to soften a bit too much, put them in the freezer and rest easy, knowing this shake is in your near future.

YIELD: 4 SHAKES

12 to 15 fresh Mission figs, halved and frozen

1 cup ice cubes

1 cup almond or coconut milk, or more as needed

1/8 teaspoon vanilla extract or paste

Pinch ground nutmeg

Combine all the ingredients in a blender or food processor and process until smooth. Add more almond or coconut milk if necessary to achieve the desired consistency.

DARK CHOCOLATE TOFU PUDDING

Pudding from scratch is delicious, but it involves a lot of standing over the stove, constant whisking, and fretting over the pudding developing a "skin" in the refrigerator. Make this easy, tofu-based, very rich chocolate pudding instead in about 5 minutes and with minimal mess. Even the tofu-averse will love it, because, thanks to the hefty quantity of chocolate, cocoa powder, and other flavorings, not one iota of tofu flavor is detectable.

YIELD: 4 SERVINGS

One 14-ounce package soft silken tofu, drained

1 cup dark chocolate chips or chunks, melted

¼ cup unsweetened cocoa powder

3 to 4 tablespoons maple syrup or honey, or more to taste

¼ teaspoon kosher salt

1 teaspoon vanilla extract or paste

Whipped cream (dairy or plant based), shaved chocolate, and/or flaky sea salt, for garnish (optional)

Combine the tofu, melted chocolate, cocoa powder, maple syrup, salt, and vanilla in a blender or food processor. Purée until very creamy and smooth.

Scrape the pudding into dessert cups or bowls. The pudding may be served immediately, but the texture will be better after at least an hour in the refrigerator.

Serve garnished with whipped dairy or coconut cream, shaved chocolate, and/or flaky sea salt, if desired.

CARAMEL SHORTBREAD BARS

These bars are a playful, vegan-friendly take on a very popular candy bar that also features shortbread, caramel, and a chocolate coating. Despite their lack of dairy, they are so rich and decadent that they need nothing other than a faint sprinkle of flaky salt to garnish.

YIELD: 6–8 SERVINGS

FOR THE SHORTBREAD

1 cup blanched almond flour (not almond meal)

⅛ teaspoon kosher salt

2 tablespoons granulated or coconut sugar

2 tablespoons unsalted plant-based butter, or virgin coconut oil, melted

1 tablespoon water

FOR THE CARAMEL

1 cup Toasty, Salty Date Caramel (page 191)

FOR THE CHOCOLATE COATING

⅔ cup semisweet or dark chocolate chips or chunks

1 tablespoon coconut oil

A few pinches flaky sea salt

NOTE: Be sure to budget time for chilling the caramel and chocolate layers: They won't set up correctly if you try to put them together warm.

Preheat the oven to 350°F. Grease a 9-by-5-inch loaf pan or line it with parchment paper. If you don't have a loaf pan, use an 8-by-8-inch baking dish.

To make the shortbread: In a medium mixing bowl, combine the almond flour, kosher salt, sugar, butter, and water. Mix with a fork or your hands until the mixture is very crumbly. Use your hands to press the almond flour mixture into the prepared pan. Optionally, use the bottom of a small glass to smooth the top even more. Prick the top of the almond dough all over with the tines of a fork.

Bake the shortbread for 20 to 25 minutes, until lightly browned (the edges will be browner). Remove from the oven and let cool in the pan. Once cool, use a spatula or knife to very gently loosen the cookie layer from the pan, just to ensure it isn't sticking (this isn't necessary if you used parchment paper).

To make the caramel: If the caramel is cold, warm for 15 to 20 seconds in the microwave or in a pot over low heat, just until it becomes easily pourable. Pour the caramel over the top of the cookie layer, using an offset spatula or rubber scraper to gently encourage it across the expanse of the cookie. Put the pan in the freezer for at least 20 minutes to allow the caramel to become very firm.

To make the chocolate coating: Just before you take the pan out of the freezer, melt the chocolate in a double boiler or in a microwave-safe bowl on high power for 1 to 2 minutes, stirring every 30 seconds. Stir in the coconut oil.

Pour the chocolate over the chilled cookie and caramel layers, using an offset spatula or rubber scraper to smooth it. Finish with a sprinkle of flaky salt.

Return the shortbread to the freezer for at least 25 minutes. When ready to cut, gently lift the entire bar out of the loaf pan and onto a cutting board. Use a very sharp or serrated knife to cut it into 1-inch-thick slices (if using an 8-by-8 pan, cut into squares) and serve immediately. Store leftovers in an airtight container in the freezer.

TOASTY, SALTY DATE CARAMEL

Most date caramel recipes call for blending dates with coconut milk and maybe vanilla and a little salt, then calling it a day. There's nothing wrong with that, but because nothing in it is actually caramelized, it isn't quite enough like the real thing to fully scratch the caramel sauce itch. This take on date caramel combines the best elements of both vegan date caramel and classic sugar caramel. It starts like regular date caramel in a blender, but instead of using just enough coconut milk to encourage the dates to blend, an entire can is poured in. Once puréed, the mixture will seem far too loose, but once cooked, the sugars do in fact caramelize. The final sauce is unlike anything you've ever tasted. Pour it over ice cream, dip cookies and fruit into it, use it in recipes calling for caramel (like the Caramel Shortbread Bars on page 188), or eat it straight out of the jar with the biggest spoon you can find.

YIELD: 6–8 SERVINGS

15 Medjool dates, pitted

1 tablespoon raw cashews

1½ cups full-fat coconut milk (from a can), plus more as needed

2 teaspoons vanilla extract or paste

¼ teaspoon kosher salt, or more to taste

Put the dates and cashews in a bowl and cover with boiling water. Cover the bowl with a lid (a plate or pan lid works well) and let the dates soak for 15 minutes. Drain the dates and cashews and put them into a blender or food processor. Add the coconut milk. Blend on high speed until very smooth (don't be afraid to let the blender go for a minute or two if necessary).

Pour the date-coconut mixture into a small pot over medium-high heat. Bring the caramel up to a simmer and allow to cook, stirring and scraping the sides frequently with a rubber spatula or wooden spoon, for 7 to 8 minutes, until quite thickened. If you would like a thinner caramel, add a bit more coconut milk.

Turn off the heat and add the vanilla and salt to the pot. Stir well. Taste for salt, adding more as desired. The caramel will be easier to pour when warm, so it's best to either use it immediately or store it in an airtight container in the fridge for up to a week, then warm in a pot on the stove or in the microwave just before using.

AFTERPARTY

IDEAS AND RESOURCES

When you're deep in the flow of the music, maybe dancing so hard you sweat through your clothes, singing along with the band at the top of your lungs, the end of a Grateful Dead show seems miles away, but alas, eventually the music does indeed end, the band makes their exit, and the lights come back on.

But the magic of the Grateful Dead doesn't end with the last note of a show's final song. Think of the recipes in this book as a way to conjure the energy of a Dead show through food anytime you find yourself hungry—whether for lunch, dinner, or just a little taste of kindness.

DAVE'S PICKS

David Lemieux is the legacy manager and audiovisual archivist for the Grateful Dead for whom he has worked since 1999, managing the band's tape archive, producing scores of album releases, hosting more than 6,000 radio shows, and appearing on many podcasts about the Dead. He is perhaps best known for the *Dave's Picks* series, albums of live Grateful Dead shows he selects and produces. Lemieux is also a longtime vegetarian-turned-vegan and avid plant-based cook. Below you'll find his personally curated list of favorite recipes from this book.

TROLLEY CAR

ACKNOWLEDGMENTS

Many thanks:

To my wonderful editor, Edward Ash-Milby, for your wise words, excellent insight, and friendship. I'm so lucky to have you!

To my agent, Richard Abate, for your guidance and faith in me for all these years.

To Mary Lagier and Kendra Aronson, for bringing this book to life with your gorgeous photos.

To Hannah Carande, for your attention to detail and hard work.

To the whole team at Weldon Owen, Insight Editions, and Simon & Schuster, for all you did to bring this book into the world.

To David Lemieux, for your encyclopedic knowledge of all things Grateful Dead, vegan cooking prowess, and enthusiasm for this project. You made the process of writing this cookbook infinitely more rewarding and fun.

To Mollie Katzen, for your friendship, collaboration, and beautiful foreword. The imprint you've made on food and on the world underpins so much of this book, and the imprint you've made on me as a writer, artist, and cook is part of all that I do.

To Judy Ng at Warner Music Group, for the helpful (and very prompt!) responses to my many queries.

To Jordan Auleb, Amir Bar-Lev, and Alex Mamlet, for sharing your Grateful Dead food memories with me. They were extremely helpful as I built the book's recipe list and deliciously fun to bring to life in my kitchen!

To Joe Eglash, my BFF-in-law and one of the few people with whom I actually enjoy sharing a kitchen, for your time, attention, recommendations, and perfect playlists.

To my culinary bestie, Jessica Nolan, for your support, brainstorming sessions, and, of course, all the cookies.

To my sweet father-in-law, Alan, we miss you terribly, and I wish I could give you a copy of this cookbook so you could tease me about how many vegetables are in it.

To Mom, Dad, Jeremy, Jen, Haran, and Kathy, for your love and steadfast support as I worked on this book.

To Anna and Sasha, my favorite two people to feed. I'm so lucky to be your mom.

And to my amazing husband, cheerleader, music educator, dishwasher, coffee maker, and enthusiastic devourer of everything I cook (vegetables, legumes, nuts, and/or seeds or otherwise). There's no one else I'd rather do life with.

APPENDIX

Resources for the Home Cook
Kind Kitchen Resources
Online Grocery Stores, Bulk Ingredients, and Spices

Azure Standard: Bulk organic ingredients like grains, beans, spices, flours, and pantry staples. Excellent for homesteaders and zero-waste enthusiasts.
Website: azurestandard.com

Bulk Apothecary: Bulk ingredients for cooking and baking, including oils, flours, and spices. Great for zero-waste kitchens.
Website: bulkapothecary.com

Frontier Co-op: Bulk organic spices, herbs, and seasonings. Available online and in many natural food stores.
Website: frontiercoop.com

iHerb: Natural and organic groceries, spices, bulk ingredients, and specialty vegan/vegetarian items.
Website: iherb.com

Imperfect Foods/Misfits Market: Affordable, organic produce, pantry items, and sustainable groceries that help reduce food waste.
Websites: imperfectfoods.com, misfitsmarket.com

Mountain Rose Herbs: Organic, sustainably sourced herbs, spices, teas, and cooking ingredients in bulk. Offers refillable options.
Website: mountainroseherbs.com

Nuts.com: High-quality bulk ingredients, including nuts, seeds, dried fruit, flours, and spices. Perfect for zero-waste kitchens.
Website: nuts.com

Public Goods: A minimalist, zero-waste-focused retailer offering vegan-friendly pantry staples, oils, and organic products.
Website: publicgoods.com

San Francisco Herb Co.: Bulk spices, teas, herbs, and botanicals shipped nationwide from San Francisco, California.
Website: sfherb.com

Spice House: Premium, sustainably sourced spices, herbs, and blends for cooking. Offers refillable glass jars and bulk purchases.
Website: thespicehouse.com

Thrive Market: Organic, non-GMO, and vegan/vegetarian pantry staples, including bulk grains, oils, snacks, and condiments.
Website: thrivemarket.com

Vitacost: Affordable organic pantry staples, vegan snacks, superfoods, and supplements.
Website: vitacost.com

ZERO-WASTE KITCHEN TOOLS AND PRODUCTS

ONLINE ZERO-WASTE STORES

PACKAGE FREE SHOP: Offers zero-waste kitchen essentials like beeswax wraps, stainless steel containers, bamboo utensils, and compost bins.
Website: packagefreeshop.com

EARTHHERO: Sells sustainable kitchen tools such as reusable storage bags, compostable sponges, and plastic-free dishware.
Website: earthhero.com

ECOROOTS: Provides zero-waste kitchen products, including biodegradable sponges, silicone food storage, and reusable containers.
Website: ecoroots.us

LIFE WITHOUT PLASTIC: Focuses on sustainable and plastic-free kitchen tools like stainless steel food containers, utensils, and brushes.
Website: lifewithoutplastic.com

ZERO WASTE STORE: Offers eco-friendly dish brushes, bamboo products, compost bins, and zero-waste food storage options.
Website: zerowastestore.com

INDEX

D

E

ABOUT THE AUTHOR

Gabi Moskowitz is the founder of BrokeAssGourmet.com, an award-winning website about inexpensive gourmet cooking. She's written five cookbooks and produced Freeform's *Young & Hungry*, a situation comedy based on her life and writing. Gabi lives in Marin County with her husband and daughters.

weldon**owen**
an imprint of Insight Editions
P.O. Box 3088
San Rafael, CA 94912
www.weldonowen.com

CEO Raoul Goff
SVP Group Publisher Jeff McLaughlin
VP Publisher Roger Shaw
Executive Editor Edward Ash-Milby
Assistant Editor Kayla Belser
Managing Editor Michelle Hope
VP Creative Chrissy Kwasnik
Art Director & Designer Megan Sinead Bingham
Production Designer Jean Hwang
VP Manufacturing Alix Nicholaeff
Senior Production Manager Joshua Smith
Strategic Production Planner Lina s Palma-Temena

Cover Art Justin Helton (StatusSerigraph.com)
Photographer Mary Lagier
Food Stylist Kendra Aronson
Food Stylist Assistants Abby Ahlgrim, Hannah Brooke, and Shea Somma

Weldon Owen would also like to thank Bev Miller, Karen Levy, and Mary Cassells.

ISBN: 979-8-88674-283-1

Manufactured in China by Insight Editions
10 9 8 7 6 5 4 3 2 1

REPLANTED PAPER

Insight Editions, in association with Roots of Peace, will plant two trees for each tree used in the manufacturing of this book. Roots of Peace is an internationally renowned humanitarian organization dedicated to eradicating land mines worldwide and converting war-torn lands into productive farms and wildlife habitats. Roots of Peace will plant two million fruit and nut trees in Afghanistan and provide farmers there with the skills and support necessary for sustainable land use.